Pelican Books
Children in Prima

GH00732874

Richard Mabey was born in 1941 and found himself
in the education business after graduating from
Oxford. He spent two years as a lecturer in social
studies in a College of Further Education and one
year freelance writing and lecturing before joining
the education division of Penguins, where he has
been an editor since 1966. He was responsible for
creating CONNEXIONS and for directing the Penguin
Primary Project, which embodies many of the ideas
expressed in this book.

He is currently spending half his time writing
on the subjects dearest to his heart, natural history
and the countryside. He has written a survey of the
edible wild plants of Great Britain, entitled *Food for
Free*, and is working on two books on the wildlife
and ecology of urban areas.

He is a frequent broadcaster and his other publications include *The Pop Process*, *Behind the Scene*,
and articles in *New Society*, *The Countryman*,
and *Teachers World*.

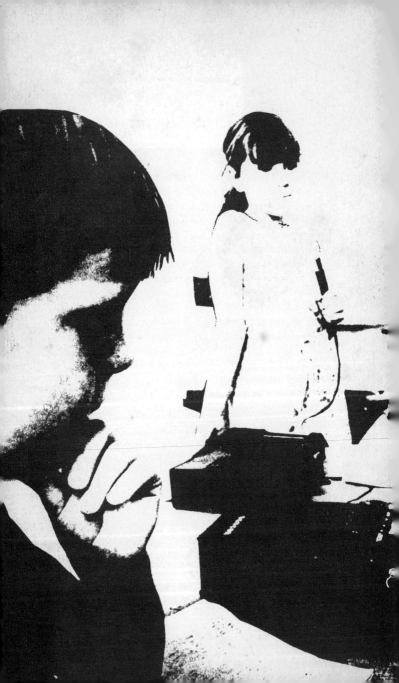

Children in Primary School

The Learning Experience

Richard Mabey

Penguin Books

Penguin Books Ltd, Harmondsworth,
Middlesex, England
Penguin Books Inc., 7110 Ambassador Road,
Baltimore, Maryland 21207, U.S.A.
Penguin Books Australia Ltd, Ringwood,
Victoria, Australia

First published 1972

Copyright © Richard Mabey, 1972
Made and printed in Great Britain by
Cox & Wyman Ltd, London, Reading and Fakenham
Set in Intertype Lectura

For Maz

Contents

Preface

This book is chiefly concerned with the contribution that one particular section of the outside world can make to the work of the modern primary school. I ought to make it clear that the book, too, is written from a vantage point outside the school walls: that of the producer of educational material. Nevertheless during its preparation I had the opportunity to make frequent visits to schools, in my capacity as editorial director of the Penguin Primary Project. I am grateful to Charles Clark, director of Penguin Education, for allowing me to make double use of my time in this way.

I must thank, too, the many headteachers, teachers, and children who not only welcomed me into their schools and classrooms, but lent me so much of their time and experience. Especial thanks in this connection to Alan Cummins, J. H. Embling, Vernon Hale, Ken Hoy, Wendla Kernig, Sheila Lane, David Lindsay, Ted Orsborn, Donald Ward and Derek Waters.

Sue Jarrett deciphered and typed up my patchwork manuscript, and Christine Vincent gave selflessly, as usual, of her time and imagination in helping track down and select the illustrations.

Finally I must thank Margery Morris and the BBC for permission to quote an extract from the schools radio programme 'Children in the Bush' and the National Committee for Audio-Visual Aids in Education for permission to quote extracts from 'Experiments in Television'.

R.M.

Part One

Context

On one of my first visits to a modern primary school I was put in the care of two urbane eight-year-olds. They'd clearly been in the guide business for some time, but they tolerated my rather stupid questions without the slightest show of patronization. The purpose of my visit had been to look at the battery of audio-visual equipment with which their school was splendidly endowed. But in the end it was this display of confident nonchalance by the children that impressed me most. They carried out their assignment perfectly, to be sure: they played me one of their taped documentaries, demonstrated how a bulky 16mm sound projector was loaded with film, and explained the logic behind the complicated card index to the film and recorded items in their library. But there was none of the wide-eyed amazement that children are reputed to show when faced with the wonders of the Electronic Age, no gleeful 'goshes' or manic tinkering. Later, I asked them about the function of a low building at the edge of the school field. 'Oh, that's Infants,' one replied. 'I don't know how they manage. They haven't even got a television.'

The media (I'm not calling them the *mass* media here for if they have one quality in common in schools it is their capacity to facilitate private, individual learning) are now well and truly involved with our young children's school lives. So numerous are the gadgets available for educating through the ear and eye that many larger schools now have full-time audio-visual experts. In part this growth has been

1. 'I imagine he will be just an ordinary, normal, scruffy, little boy. You know what small boys are like at that age – a lollipop in their pockets and their socks round their ankles.'
A spokesman for Prince Edward's pre-preparatory school.

a spin-off of the expansion of the communications industry. Diversification is a fashionable policy for growing businesses, and the educational market, with its vast captive audience, was an inevitable target. But the school system was far from unhappy about being wooed in this way. There were compelling educational reasons, some rooted in necessity, some in policy, why the wholesale entry of the media into the schools could be a boon: the increasing sophistication and confidence of children in the handling of these devices; the chronic shortage of teachers, which puts a palliative value on self-instructional aids – and the growing belief in individualized learning, which positively relishes them.

So the gadgets have moved in. Where there was once nothing more than the teacher dispensing wisdom verbally or on the blackboard, there are now closed-circuit television networks, hi-fi record players, light-rooms, film-loop projectors, portable cassette tape recorders and books in full

2. One classroom in a well-endowed junior school. The children are operating all the equipment quite unassisted. Notice the lean of that head on the closed-circuit TV screen; the eight-year-old presenter already has the confidence of a newsreader.

3. The light-room at Sunfield School, Worcs. This is a device used in schools for mentally handicapped children in which individual children are given what amounts to a personalized light show. The continuously changing pattern of lights projected on to the walls helps not only to relax the children, but to develop their perceptive and imaginative powers.

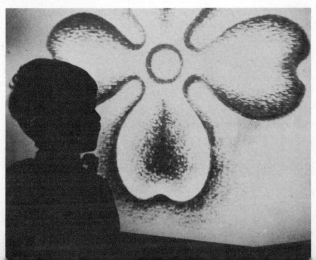

colour produced for no other purpose than to be taken apart. But if the children, like my two guides, accept these devices as a thoroughly natural part of their environment, the reaction in adult quarters has been less whole-hearted. Teachers brought up on more traditional methods see themselves being made obsolete – and by machines at that. Many parents are also suspicious; and why not? If the only television they have a chance to watch is the evening medley of crass entertainment, it is understandable that they wonder if that broadcast during school hours is any different. There has been no attempt to explain to these parents the nature and purpose of the new devices which the schools are placing in their children's hands. No wonder that so many see in this development confirmation of their belief that modern primary schooling is frivolous and indulgent.

These particular fears can be easily allayed with a little information. One of the things I have tried to do in the second half of this book is to give this, and to explain how and why these devices are playing such an important role in schools.

But there are other, more serious worries. If some parents see the intrusion of the media as part and parcel of the decline in primary school standards, there are many more, plus a goodly number of teachers, who fear that the spread of educational technology may threaten everything they cherish about primary education. There is no doubt that the modern primary school has a distinct and sympathetic image. It is a place of warmth and security, where the growth of affectionate relationships between adult and child has the same priority as academic learning. The surrender to economically desirable patterns of learning has been happily postponed for a few years and the children can explore their own personalities and roots of the learning process with a freedom and intensity they will only experience again if they go to university. Experience is in fact a key notion. Think of the props of a primary school and the first things to come to your mind will almost certainly be the great flood of materials used to involve the children's senses: frog spawn, finger paints. gerbils, egg boxes and sand.

To this friendly, tactile, free-ranging world, the on-off buttons and teaching machines of the educational technologists do seem to present a sinister contrast. Aren't their chief characteristics impersonality, second-handedness and programming – just those qualities that the progressive primary school has been fighting against? This seems to me to be the key question about the use of the new devices in schools, and it is the one I have tried to answer in this short book. What I hope to argue is that not only have the characteristics of the media been misunderstood, but that far from threatening the basic aims of modern primary education, they are of the greatest help in facilitating them. But one thing must be tackled at the outset. The new teaching devices are no more and no less machines than the human vocal cords. When they're not being used they are indeed comparatively lifeless. But when they 'speak' it has to be a human voice that animates them. A record of a professional musician can give the child an experience he might never have in the 'real' world – especially if his teacher sensitively and deliberately takes a back seat, and allows him to confront the music face to face. A set of slides may be the combined work of a dozen people: artists, photographers, librarians, designers and teachers. Only with an exceedingly rose-tinted view of the purity of face-to-face relationships could such products be seen as devoid of humanity.

I think two important points emerge here. First, that it is crucial to distinguish between the machines, the 'hardware' as they're now referred to in educational jargon, and what goes into them: the 'software'. The chief educational value of a film projector is that through it a child has access to films. But this is not its only value. The device itself, used individually, may enable a child to go through a learning experience in his own way and at his own speed that he previously had to endure as a lowest common denominator in a class of forty. Inside the school environment the machine may also carry a powerful charge of authenticity for the child; these, after all, are the objects through which news and hard facts are piped into their homes. This can of course be as dangerous to a child's gullibility as it can be useful as a motivation. But one way round this danger may be to exploit another virtue of the new media: that it is entirely possible for the children to produce the software themselves.

The second point is closely related to this. It is impossible to discuss the implications of these new channels of learning outside the context of the overall blurring of distinctions between formal education inside the school and informal in the outside world. I suggested above that a set of educational slides is probably the combined work of a dozen people not directly concerned with primary education. This pooling of skills, and the implicit notion that the education of young children is the business of the whole community, is reflected in every aspect of the modern primary school's work. Parents increasingly come into school to help informally with the teaching and with the maintenance of equipment – and the children return the gesture by putting on concerts for the elderly.

The new channels of communication in the primary classroom enable an even larger community to participate in the business of education. Marcel Marceau, on a film loop, is now a member of the teaching staff. Exotic bird calls from archives of recorded sound can become part of the school's resources. A whole battery of specialized skills and materials is increasingly at the disposal of the primary teacher – who is thus happily freed from the onus of pretending to be Sir Mortimer Wheeler, and able to concentrate on her chosen business of helping children to learn.

But perhaps the most significant aspect of the merging process is less literal than this. Primary school children are growing up in a communications environment vastly different from the one which shaped their parents and teachers. The transistor radio and midget tape recorder are now as common as birthday presents as bicycles and paint-boxes once were. Children take it for granted that *The News at Ten* is where you get the facts, not a newspaper, and that what is seen is to be believed. They value, rightly or wrongly, the visual, the colourful, the instant and the sensational.

Unless the primary schools acknowledge this, and begin to talk to children through the channels that are now a natural part of their lives, they will run the risk of becoming out-dated, second-string communicators. That wise document on primary education, the Plowden Report, was very clear about this:

There is a further reason for introducing more aids into school. Television is now, as films and sound broadcasting have long been, a part of ordinary life to which children are accustomed. It has even been described as 'a rival system of education'. Children must be taught to use it profitably and to associate it with learning as well as with entertainment. This point of view has to be balanced with another: for the youngest children, in particular, who spend more time in front of the television set than any other age group, there is a particular need for the school to provide direct experiences when all the senses come into play. In this way precision, associations and meaning can be added to what is seen and heard on television.[1]

1. *Children and their Primary Schools*, HMSO, 1966.

19

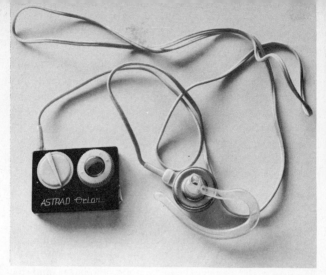

4. A miniature radio, not much bigger than a postage stamp, and with an earpiece easily camouflaged by long hair. It will pick up most stations *except* Radio One.

5.

In all these ways the development of the new media is inextricably bound up with the changing relationships between the primary school and the outside world. This raises questions about the very definition of the primary school. Where does the school end and the community begin? How do formal and informal education differ? Should the school be challenging the standards and techniques of the mass media or copying them? We are brought back to the central theme of this book: do the new media – undeniably creatures of informal learning and the outside world – pose any sort of threat to the basic tenets of organized primary schooling?

A Model

A few hundred yards from my office there is a toyshop window display that is a compact symbol of what I have been discussing. There are precious few toys in the sense I understood them as a child: a few tops poked away in the corner, an antediluvian water pistol looking positively gentle amongst its Cold War descendants.

But up close to the window are box upon box of junior technological wizardry. There are telescopes for the moon and microscopes for blood; electrical construction kits; chunky models of jeeps, detailed down to the last wheel nut – all of them packaged with crisp and compellingly realistic illustrations.

Inevitably many of the items reflect children's traditional passions for action and violence. Yet so exact and contemporary are they that they seem sinister in a way that Cowboy and Indian gear never did. The GI, in particular, would seem to be somewhat more popular over here than amongst his young compatriots. His equipment, from muzzle-loader to mobile missile firer, is the most conspicuous in the shop. You can even buy models of his current Asian enemies.

Equally, there is a clear recognition of young children's love of activity. Most of these new toys are kits of one sort or another. Admittedly, they usually demand no more of the child than the gluing together of a few pieces of pre-formed plastic; but even this needs a measure of dexterity, and the ability to perceive a whole from its parts.

But pride of place in the display goes to 'Visible Woman', a plastic mock-up of the female body in which 'you can assemble, remove, replace all organs'. The model is decidedly carnal, with full breasts and luxuriant red arteries, which are also displayed for all the world to see on the box. Yet the makers clearly expect some sort of parental mediation between this inflammatory object and their innocent offspring, for printed on the box is this note: 'Optional feature: the Miracle of Creation. Understanding female biology requires observation of those parts related to gestation. Included therefore is a separate group of components representing this phenomenon. Assembly is optional.'

I think it would be difficult to find, in one window, a more complete survey of our confused and ambiguous attitudes towards young children and their relationships with the grown-up world of war, sex and the media. The kits, for instance, are not of specially created toys. They're essentially scale models, child-sized replicas of adult-world objects. And yet the likeness must not be too discomfortingly exact; just as Visible Woman's genitals are in a sealed envelope, so there is no blood on the American serviceman.

Again, look at the small print on those smart boxes and you will usually find some direct or oblique reference to

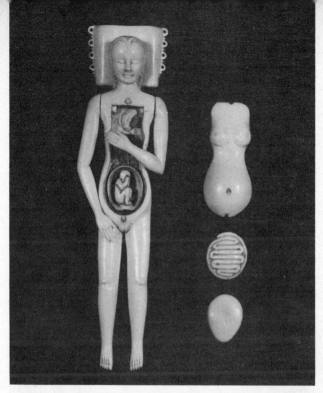

6. Visible Woman, 16th-century style. A German statuette designed to demonstrate the anatomy of pregnancy. For all our so-called permissiveness, you would be hard put to find a contemporary model as honest and unromanticized as this.

'education'. (VW 'turns hobbies into science', and the handbook is written by 'medical authorities'.) It is a convenient salesman's word, a powerful incantation for parents worried about their children's chances in an increasingly competitive society. And yet here these things are in a *toy* shop, being bought as Christmas presents at least under the pretence of being fun.

One senses behind all this a major confusion in our attitudes towards young children. Are they just small adults or

23

a special type of person? Is childhood something to be hung on to or grown out of? Will children learn enough if left to their own devices? Will they learn too *much*? Most parents, I think, initiate their children into the universe of technology with something of a nostalgic sigh. They are bound to give their kids the best opportunities, to 'do right by them'; yet – isn't it a little sad that they don't play much any more those secret, fantastical games, that they cannot escape the Vietnam war on the newsreels, that much of the innocence and magic seems to have left their lives?

Of course, it hasn't really; and it is one of the saddest consequences of the 'media-gap' that many parents cannot

7. Mass circulation.

see this. Their children have grown up with the media and cope with them almost intuitively. The parents come to them as strangers, and try to evaluate them by the standards of their own education and culture. So they see only the soulless hardware, not the age-old child-like qualities of mystery, invention and fantasy being distilled from these seemingly improbable materials. If this were not so there would be real cause for alarm, for a modern industrial society must look to its children as perhaps the last guardians of these qualities. But they rarely let us down. They have marvellous reserves of imagination and irreverence that can time and again give them the last laugh over the operators. They were at it as early as the mid fifties, with the 'Davy Crockett' craze.

Davy Crockett was a ballad about an American frontiersman of legendary powers that formed part of Walt Disney Production's publicity for a film of the same name. The campaign associated with this film was perhaps at that time the most ambitious and hard-hitting ever aimed at an exclusively primary audience. There were Davy Crockett hunting spears, fishing rods, transfers and nougat bars. Most popular were the imitation coon-skin hats. But the song remained the pivot of the cult and was the item of the package on which kids exercised most of their ingenuity. Into the playground went the official lyrics, processed and innocuous; out came the racy backstreet vernacular, full of clever puns and word-play:

> Born on a table top in Joe's Cafe,
> The dirtiest place in the U.S.A.,
> Fell in love with Doris Day,
> Thought he could sing like Johnnie Ray.
> > Davy, Davy Crewcut
> > King of the Teddy boys.[1]

1. Quoted in *The Lore and Language of Schoolchildren*, Iona and Peter Opie, Oxford, 1959.

8. The trappings may be different, but the game's the same.

So the media are close to the nub of our present confusion about children's identity. They are part of a riddle so involved that I would not presume to tackle it head-on: how do we preserve what is essentially valuable about childhood, whilst educating our children to cope with an increasingly *adult* culture, and using necessarily as part of this process those communications media that belong to the adult world but seem to be understood most naturally by children?

The Primary Socializer

So what of the modern primary school itself? What are its distinctive characteristics, and in particular those that might be most vulnerable to – or most assisted by – the new

9.

media? To understand the way that primary schools are developing we must look briefly at our changing notions of the way children learn, and indeed of what they *are*.

At the age of five, the human child has a brain which has reached nine tenths of its adult weight. He can stand upright, walk straight, copy the characters of his name. If he has not come from a deprived background he will have a spoken vocabulary of about 2,000 words. There will be no more great or sudden changes in his physical development until he reaches puberty; as a biological specimen he has arrived at 'the latency period'. Yet during the next seven years he will pass through all the social changes which are important to him as a prospective member of an organized society. He will make friends with other children and with adults besides his parents. He will begin to distinguish between his fantasy life and the real world, and to develop a rough and ready moral sense. He will rely less and less on immediate experience for his judgements, and begin to adopt the abstract theoretical framework of adult thinking. With any luck, he will achieve that peculiar distinction of civilized man and learn to read.

It is at just this crucial period in his development as a human being that the law requires his education at home to be supplemented. For six hours a day, 180 days a year, the moulding of the young child, his mother's familiar, must pass into the hands of strangers. It is a momentous stage in the child's life, a real *rite de passage* between private and public existence.

During these years his emotional and intellectual landscape changes radically. Everything he does inside the social framework of the school is an expression of these changes. When he joins in playground games he is rehearsing an elaborate array of social relationships. When he does his first scientific experiments he is beginning to replace his own intuitive self-centred mental framework with a picture of a world where he is no longer in complete control, where there are areas of inevitability and of surprise.

10.

It is during these primary years, just as much as during adolescence, that the child begins to develop important adult traits. It's hardly surprising then that with a better understanding of the social development of children has come a change in their social *status*. Not many parents today would publicly declare that they hope to 'make their children in their own image'. The child is seen more and more as a viable human being in his own right, not just as a preparation for some higher state or as an appendage to his parents. He has rights and responsibilities. His activities can be meaningful and useful even in adult terms.

The implications for the primary school of this shift in attitude is that the child's formal education isn't simply looked at as a way of preparing him for adulthood. A child spends six years – maybe a twelfth of his life – at primary school; it would be criminal not to try and make this a happy and enriching time, regardless of its outcome. Another extract from the Plowden Report shows just how far this attitude has seeped into the official view of the primary school's function:

A school . . . is a community in which children learn to live first and foremost as children and not as future adults. In family life children learn to live with people of all ages. The school sets out deliberately to devise the right environment for children, to allow them to be themselves and to develop in the way and at the pace appropriate to them. It tries to equalize opportunities and to compensate for handicaps. It lays special stress on individual discovery, on first-hand experience and on opportunities for creative work. It insists that knowledge does not fall into neatly separate compartments and that work and play are not opposite but complementary. A child brought up in such an atmosphere at all stages of his education has some hope of becoming a balanced and mature adult and of being able to live in, contribute to, and to look critically at the society of which he forms a part. Not all primary schools correspond to this picture, but it does represent a general and quickening trend.

Some people, while conceding that children are happier under the modern regime and perhaps more versatile, question whether they are being fitted to grapple with the world they will enter on leaving school. The view is worth examining because it is quite widely held, but we think it rests on a misconception. It isolates the long-term objective, that of living in and serving society, and regards education as being at all stages recognizably and specifically a preparation for this. It fails to understand that the best preparation for being a happy and useful man or woman is to live fully as a child.[1]

Plowden is at pains to point out that not all primary schools 'correspond to this picture'. The report estimated that by 1967, one third of British primary schools were deeply committed to the attitude expressed in that extract, and another third had been brushed by it in some way. The report was extremely influential, and there can be little doubt that these proportions have increased in the years following its publication.

But what are the implications of this shift in attitude for what happens on the classroom floor? To respect children more as people, to urge that they should 'live fully' in school, as they may hopefully do in later life, are *moral* decisions. We must not mistake them for educational programmes based on scientific analyses of the way children learn most effectively. But schools are part of our society, and ought not to be untouched by our feelings about how children should be treated as human beings. And nothing in the great deal that educational psychologists have discovered about the way young children learn contradicts the policies these moral positions would lead us to adopt.

The importance of first-hand, sensory *experience* is the most basic of these findings. The distinguished Swiss educational psychologist, Piaget,[2] has stressed how children

1. *Children and their Primary Schools*, HMSO, 1966.
2. This short book is not really the place for a comprehensive

11. For young children the feel of the wood and the tools and the sense of one's effect upon the other are as important as the end product itself.

up to the age of about six or seven cannot begin abstract thinking until they have had direct evidence through their senses of qualities like shape, number, proportion and texture. So you will find children in most primary schools exercising their nerve endings for all they are worth.

---

survey of the theory and practice of modern primary education. For those who want this, there is nothing to beat the Plowden Report itself, 500 pages long, but every one enticingly readable. For shorter accounts of the practice, there is John Blackie's *Inside the Primary School*, HMSO, 1967, and *Children at School* CREDO, Heinemann, 1969. The key figures in the historical development of modern primary school philosophy are Froebel, Montessori, and Dewey. But the modern, more experimentally-based educationists are increasingly influential. Try *The Origins of Intellect: Piaget's Theory*, John L. Phillips, W. H. Freeman, 1969, and *The Process of Education*, Jerome Bruner, Vintage Books, 1960.

They will be squeezing polystyrene, and noticing how it seems curiously warm to the touch. The younger ones may be pouring water from tall jars into squat ones, and beginning to realize that 'biggest' does not always mean 'tallest'. The water will doubtless be spilt and the odd jar broken. Giving new experiences to growing sense organs will always be an untidy business. Sometimes, too, it is bound to be very slightly dangerous; a wise teacher will never stop a child from having one lick, at least, at some unfamiliar substance. To adults, some of these experiments may seem positively grotesque, like the gigantic model of the intestines which some children built so that they could follow on hands and knees the path taken by their dinners.

From these very physical experiences the children come to grips with the stuff from which our world is made. They are the first, vital foundations on which abstract thinking is based. And with new sensations must come new terms in which to describe them. So vocabulary is extended and a store of fresh imagery built up for the children's creative work in writing and painting.

Later the children will begin to organize these explorations more purposefully. Then we have *activity* learning, or 'learning by doing'. It is ironic that this method, the oldest educational practice of all, the counter of every master-apprentice relationship and of most informal teaching, should have taken so long to become respectable inside the formal school system. Yet now it has the backing of an impressive body of research. The principle is so obvious that it scarcely needs labouring: the best way to learn to ride a bike is to get on one and try.

But in the modern primary school, it is not just the manual skills that are learned most effectively in this way. As the American educationist Jerome Bruner has suggested,

even the best way to learn to *think* creatively is by prac-
tising doing just that, not by listening to someone else's
ready-made solutions:

> . . . intellectual activity anywhere is the same, whether at the
> frontier of knowledge or in a third-grade classroom. What a
> scientist does at his desk or in his laboratory, what a literary
> critic does in reading a poem, are of the same order as what
> anybody else does when he is engaged in like activities – if he is
> to achieve understanding. The difference is in degree, not in kind.
> The schoolboy learning physics *is* a physicist, and it is easier for
> him to learn physics behaving like a physicist than doing some-
> thing else.[1]

I think we can see here the educational counterpart of
the social respect for children as persons that I touched on
earlier.

The practical applications of this broad principle are
varied and far-reaching. At their centre lies the *discovery*
method. This is based on the assumption that children
absorb and understand ideas more readily if they discover
them for themselves, and most readily if they *need* to discover them. This is most likely to happen when the children
are carrying out work in which they are genuinely interested
and curious to find a result. So the teacher using the discovery method encourages her children to follow up questions and ambiguities which intrigue them, and if and when
they successfully find the answers to stand back and see
whether these can help towards the understanding of other
problems. Thus the child begins to engage in the classic
scientific method: experience, experiment and activity, discovery, generalization and theory.

In the primary school this type of investigation normally
happens through *project* work. Young children cannot extract problems from their context as expertly as adults. The

---

1. *The Process of Education*, Jerome Bruner, Vintage Books, 1960.

12. When the problems as well as the answers can be devised by you, learning is given a whole new dimension of seriousness and relevance.

direction of their thinking is from the real and the experienced towards the abstract. They would start a project on flight not with the inquiries about torque and lift, but because they wanted to know why men flap off the top of bridges for money, and why they invariably fall into the water. Work of this sort, based on real-life problems which mystify the children, must also step outside the orthodox subject categories. Neither the world nor children's intellects are neatly subdivided into 'scientific' and 'imaginative'.

One of the best known uses of the discovery method inside the primary school has been the Nuffield Junior

13.

Science Project. Here is a brief account of some work done by a school taking part in this project which shows how closely the discovery method, project work, and 'inter-disciplinariness' – to use that ugly word – work out together in practice. Notice especially how one topic can lead on to another equally profitable but quite unpredictable theme:

David put some sand in a plastic box, making one end dry and the other wet, and put his slug in the middle several times to see which end it would choose. ... He and the rest of his group offered their slugs a variety of foods including toadstools, lettuce, carrot and apple, to see which they would eat. The children suddenly realized that although they could see where the slugs had been eating a piece of food, they had no idea of how they ate. Therefore they placed one slug on a piece of transparent acetate film so they could watch it from below as it ate. Tests were also made to find out whether slugs could smell and see.

The children used hand lenses to examine the slugs. The respiratory aperture in the mantle of a large slug was soon identified and the pupils were also most interested in the tentacles and their sensitivity to touch, and made detailed sketches.

The children measured a slug when it was contracted and when it was extended, and then made drawings of it in both positions. It occurred to them that human beings could also extend and contract themselves, though in a different way, so they used tinted cardboard, jointed with paper fasteners, to make a model man who could be stretched out and curled up. This led to work on joints, bones and muscles.

Next they timed how long it took a snail to travel an inch and calculated that at a constant speed it would take twenty-two days to cover a mile. Christopher and David wondered whether slugs moved in different ways over different surfaces, so they persuaded one to cross sand, soil, grit, pebbles, glass, and other surfaces to see what happened. They concluded that the surface made no difference, for it used its slime on all of them and moved in the same way. They noticed that when a slug travelling over a desk crossed a crack, the slime trail continued over it forming a bridge of slime. Baby slugs made yellow slime, while adults' was whitish or colourless.[1]

But it would be wrong of me to suggest that all primary teachers accept these ideas uncritically. Some believe that only the very bright children ever 'discover' anything when learning is organized in this way; that what they do find out is usually trivial and irrelevant, and that the whole exercise is taking up time which could be more usefully given over to drill in the fundamental skills of arithmetic, grammar and spelling. I want to look at these worries, not only because they are shared by many parents brought up inside formal schools, but because the question of what *are* the fundamental skills on which later learning can be built is crucial to understanding the value of the media in schools.

1. *Nuffield Junior Science. Teacher's Guide 2*, Collins, 1967.

One of the most vocal critics of the new methods is Stuart Froome, himself a primary headteacher, who has written a book called *Why Tommy Isn't Learning*.[1] He has this to say of the discovery method:

Rousseau, who had no scientific training and so was ill-qualified to speak on the subject, said of his Emile, 'Let him not be taught science, let him discover it', and it would seem that this strange advice is being largely followed by educationists today.

What is stranger is that this advice should itself be thought strange. For without people 'discovering' we should have no science at all. As Jerome Bruner, refining Rousseau's prescription in the light of his own research, says, the best way of learning science is to be a scientist. Why should a child not be capable of this? After all, he is not a member of a different species. He has the same basic faculties as an adult, though some of them may be undeveloped and others in a state of decay. It is his special mixture that makes him a child, not the possession of some uniquely childish cognitive system which needs to be fed intellectual babyfood. The blend is really the opposite of an adult's – strong powers of imagination but comparatively untried reasoning abilities. If the nourishing of the former is a difficult and thankless task in a society hostile to the imagination, the second just needs practice – at the real thing. We are back with Plowden: 'the best preparation for being a happy and useful man or woman is to live fully as a child'.

But those who are worried about primary schooling are not impressed by displays of 'full living' and free-wheeling (though maybe high-powered) 'discovery' work. They suspect these imprecise terms may be used to give an aura of importance to a jumble of activity that has no direction,

1. Tom Stacey Books, 1970.

purpose or educational value at all. How, with work of this sort, can you maintain *standards*? After all, everyone has their own definition of the full life. And an original discovery to one child may be a hackneyed irrelevance to his teacher. At least with the old ways of arithmetic and spelling you could *tell* when a child was learning. Stuart Froome says:

At the turn of the century, and for the first twenty years of this one, most children left school well grounded in reading, writing and arithmetic, and for good measure they also had a sound knowledge of history, geography, nature study and scripture. They had also been taught to sing and to do physical exercises, and for practical work the girls had been instructed in needlework and the boys in woodwork. Above all, however, they had learnt through firm discipline the value of effort and concentration in acquiring the basic skills necessary for a fuller education.

There were no doubt faults in the early elementary system of education. Size of classes, poor accommodation and shortage of materials dictated a rigidity of method and conformity of outlook which in these days would not be considered desirable, but the efficiency of the system cannot be contested. The great majority of the children were turned out into the world at fourteen years of age able to write a simple letter with correct spelling, punctuation and grammatical construction; they were good readers, and they were reasonably accurate in dealing with the British system of money, weights and measures. Moreover, the clever ones could, through scholarship awards, pass on to secondary schools and the university.[1]

Now it may indeed be true that standards in arithmetical dexterity and formal grammar have diminished during the last fifty years. But so have those in alchemy and the making of samplers, and very few voices are raised in protest. I'm not of course denying the obvious practical importance of arithmetic and spelling, or indeed the fact that, beyond a

1. *Why Tommy Isn't Learning*, Stuart Froome, Tom Stacey Books, 1970.

certain stage, young children's learning will be severely held up until they have mastered these skills. But this is not the same as insisting that these are the *basic* skills on which future learning must be based. Nor can we confidently state that they are essential to success in life after school. Their relevance to survival in the larger world seems to become less by the day. An ability to see through visual propaganda, run a committee meeting, speak confidently on the phone, choose your food wisely, have little to do with how exquisitely you can construct a business letter. Paul Goodman's comment that with current standards of advertising it could be a positive advantage to be illiterate, was not made frivolously. And it was not the children drilled in 'the British system of money' who romped through the decimal changeover; they were stuck at base twelve. It was those brought up on New Maths and on the *ideas* behind counting who were able to swop effortlessly one system for another.

I find disturbing undertones in Stuart Froome's vision of an education system of incontestable efficiency 'turning out' children into the market-place. Is education really nothing more than a machine for manufacturing woodworkers and clerks and shop assistants – the only possible fates awaiting average children under this system? Why should they be excluded from the more exciting, intangible, abstract reaches of learning, which might help them escape, or at the very least, have richer daydreams? Because these are intellectual icing, special treats reserved 'for the clever ones [who] pass on to secondary schools and the university'?

I think that here we are at the heart of the mistake which the traditionalists are making in attacking the new methods, and also at the fundamental theoretical argument for the use of the media in primary schools. The question at issue is the nature of 'primary' – that is, basic – education. Is the best foundation for the future intellectual growth the traditional skills of arithmetic and grammar, or an ability to think critically and creatively? Can you do the second before you have a grounding in the first?

As we have seen, the traditionalist's answer is a very clear 'no'. But I believe they have been guilty of failing to distinguish between 'primary' in the logical sense and 'primary' in the psychological sense. Letters, sentences, grammatical rules are certainly the basic (primary) abstractions into

14. The primary experience of height. These nine-year-olds can measure the height of their school building quite accurately with an improvised clinometer. But the manual operation of holding that rather bulky instrument, sextant style, gives also a very tangible understanding of the meaning of height.

which we adults have broken down our language. But does this mean that they are also the initial (primary) units through which a child begins to experience language? This is a difficult point, so let me give a corny but homely analogy. The primary materials out of which we build our houses are bricks and mortar. But if we wanted a child to understand what a house was and how it worked we wouldn't begin with bricklaying lessons. The child would first need to grasp the *idea* of an environment specially built to provide for certain basic human needs. The natural development of his understanding would be from his own home, through elemental shelters like upturned cars and hollow trees, to tents and shacks. (As L. C. Taylor has said, 'the child in the primary school recapitulates essential and universal discoveries from centuries of civilization'.)[1] Only when he had grasped in broad terms why and how men build dwellings, could bricklaying lessons be anything more than meaningless technical training.

The development of children's understanding of the world is from the whole to the part. They learn to communicate first with bold undifferentiated sounds and gestures and only later begin to form words. They understand 'names' before 'letters'. Their first mathematical experiences are of shape and size, not of multiplication. To insist that children can only progress once they have learned the arbitrary rules by which adults order the world is not only contrary to the way they develop psychologically, but may actually set limits on their intellectual advance. A child who has become expert in putting bricks together has learned one useful trade, but precious little else. The child who has understood the concept of shelter has learned something about the relationships between man and his environment that, if we must be practical, will help him in a dozen

1. *Resources for Learning*, L. C. Taylor, Penguin Books, 1971.

occupations. If bricklaying is not one of these it may well be because he has decided this is, after all, a rather crude way of constructing a world to live in.

We are back with the media. Since many of them communicate in non-verbal terms they are immensely useful to children who are sorting out their world in terms of broad patterns and relationships. Any parents who have watched their very young children responding to the simplified forms of TV puppet characters will know this only too well. And as we will see, this is not to say that the media are not also of great value in more specific, detailed learning tasks.

The Adult–Child Co-operative

If the modern primary school is reluctant to be dogmatic about what intellectual 'standards' should be expected of our future children, it is also open-minded about the forms of social organization in which learning can take place. It sees value in co-operative learning as well as in competitive. One of the consequences of all that we have discussed so far about respect for the individual child's own interests and abilities is that they cannot do their learning inside large, homogenized classes. Sometimes they will be working completely by themselves, sometimes in small groups. Occasionally these groups may be formed out of children of similar ability. But an increasing number of schools are encouraging mixed-ability groupings, where the children are grouped on the basis of friendship, family or neighbourhood.

There has been criticism of classes organized in this way, especially the charge that they 'hold back' the brighter children. But I must say that I have never seen a school where children of any ability have suffered by being in unstreamed classes. But then I must confess to having the heretical view that it might not matter if the bright ones at least *did* suffer. We overvalue conventional intelligence and academic achievement in our society. We publicly applaud the virtues of compassion and co-operation, yet in our school system we encourage and perpetuate vicious competition, aggressiveness and selfishness. The bright child is in no danger, whatever happens. He is built for success. If he is frustrated at school he will study at home. Eventually he will end up in a society which has been modelled to accommodate his kind. The ones who will suffer are those whom he was never given an opportunity to work with or understand: the slow, the diffident, the children whose abilities do not lie in any of the areas approved by the education system.

Could anything but good come of the *controlled* frustration of these bright children? I am not pleading for a harness to be put on them, but for their learning activities to be sufficiently closely related to those of other children for them to appreciate the difficulties of learners slower than themselves. After all, every child is frustrated by school. But whoever considers the young football fanatic, who is lucky if he gets on a pitch once a week, let alone be allowed to watch a game on the school TV? Who makes provision for the conventionally dull girl who can nevertheless make the other children laugh? Why do we condone separation of children by intellectual ability when we would find abhorrent their separation by, say, the criterion of how well they mix with each other? Isn't the most demanding intellectual work really done in conditions where there are problems of frustration, human management and communication, as well as purely academic ones? These are the conditions of 'real' research just as much as of unstreamed classrooms. Mixed ability groupings have demonstrated that bright children need not be held back — even in the

15. The classroom pictured on p. 15 a few minutes later. Things go wrong here as they do in the outside world. Yet the teacher's help is not always needed; often a technically gifted boy (or girl) can come into his own as audio-visual odd-job man.

narrowest intellectual sense of that phrase – in unstreamed situations. Many primary teachers would go further and say that far from being held back every child is broadened by the mixed-ability experience. He is given a living lesson in the relationship between disciplines, between theory and practice, between knowledge and the social situation from which it develops.

And just as there is co-operation inside the school walls, there is between the school and the community outside. The school sees itself as *part* of the community, not just as a sanctuary (or a sanatorium) within it. The community makes use of the teacher's special skills, and the school makes use of the community's resources – both human and material. A group of schools in a run-down area of Liverpool have set up a reciprocal arrangement with the local shopping centre. The shops display the children's paintings on their walls, and Tesco has set up a supermarket in one of the schools for the children to gain practical experience in handling money and working out budgets.

This is reflected in the primary school's attitudes to visitors. In all the many visits I have paid to schools I have never once been made less than welcome (nor, I should add, been allowed simply to watch from the touchlines. I have been roped in to take playground duty, been appointed a temporary uncle to a seven-year-old deserter, represented one end of a dinosaur and imitated a nightjar).

There are two strands in this attitude that are particularly relevant here. The primary school has realized how closely related are the processes of effective formal learning and informal play. And it has capitalized faster than any other institution in our education system on the enormous wealth of talent that is available outside the school. The media, in a way, form the link between these two responses. They bring new ideas and new faces into the classroom through channels which are part of the child's natural learning environment.

Part Two

Uses and Opportunities

In the previous section I emphasized some of the characteristics of modern primary school learning: experience, individualized learning, activity, discovery, co-operative work.
These are not necessarily the most important characteristics, but being concerned with first-hand experience
and personal relations, they are the ones that might seem to
be the most vulnerable to the media.

In this section I want to look at the ways that educational
technology, intelligently used, can actually help with these
ways of working. In passing, I shall be describing how some
of its devices are operated and at the responses they elicit
from children.

I have not tried to be comprehensive in my coverage of
the gadgets. Ingenious new labour-saving devices for the
blackboard-bound teacher appear every month, and no
book could ever keep track of the developments. Nor have I
spent much time looking at some of the more traditional
virtues of teaching aids. Qualities like clarity and precision
can, I think, be taken as read; it was always better to use a
three-dimensional model of the semi-circular canals than
attempt to unravel them on the board.

What I have tried to do is to isolate some of the general
characteristics of audio-visual methods and to see how
these contribute to the aims detailed above.

There are two points I should make here. Firstly, that it is
misleading to think of the introduction of the new media as
the *automation* of education. The formal meaning of auto-

mation is the use of machines to replace manual labour; informally the word is associated with mass production and with removing the humanity from work as well as the drudgery. Neither meaning bears much relation to the effects of the devices we are discussing. If some of them do incidentally relieve the teacher of routine duties, they also give him the opportunity for more intensive and varied work with children who are working down their own individual paths; self-instruction does not mean learning in solitary confinement. Far from diminishing the human element in the classroom, educational technology can increase it, not just by being the vehicle for introducing more human

16. A primary-school class in 1935. Look at the children's faces and the direction of their gazes. Like their paintings on the wall they have been moulded into standardized products.

talent, but by releasing the teacher from the considerably less than human task of drilling simultaneously some thirty children. Surely this, the traditional classroom set-up, is a more pointedly close parallel of the mass production process.

It might be useful to distinguish here between two different sorts of drudgery: the tedious strings of facts and standardized techniques – the drudgery of ends; and the enforced labour of using the same mass teaching techniques in all types of situation with all types of children – the drudgery of means. There are many aids, old and new, which can help the teacher out with the former. Libraries, for instance, are somewhat better for storing detailed facts than the human brain. A three-minute film made with close-up lenses and special lighting can demonstrate dissection techniques far better than any teacher fiddling yards away from a group of craning children of motley heights and eye-sights. These are simply ways of meeting old educational objectives more efficiently. A more exciting aspect of many of the new devices is that they can service (and occasionally create) the learning objectives we discussed in the last section.

One of these situations is really the subject of my second point. The new media themselves – being part of the child's everyday world – can usually be operated by him as easily as he can 'read' their products. Any medium can therefore be used in two quite different ways in the school. It can beam information and stimuli *at* the children, who play the roles of listeners, viewers, etc; or it can be actively manipulated *by* the children, acting as producers, writers, photographers, etc. In the latter situation they have the opportunity to produce their own educational materials. The benefits of this are very great: not just the necessity of focused, purposeful research into a topic, but new insights

17. Children brought up on films, who have made them as well as viewed them, can watch adult productions with a nicely balanced mixture of scepticism and sympathy.

into the syntax of communication – and as a bonus, into the tricks used by the adults who run the communications industry. No nine-year-old who has had to edit a documentary film will ever be duped again by ill-informed shudders at 'bad taste' or 'partiality'. He knows that films are made by men, and each one bears their mark.

Experience

Second-Hand

A six-year-old boy has come into the headmistress's room for a few moments' quiet. The door is always open, and the place has come to be used as a refuge for the shyer children, and for those who want no more than a breathing space from the hurly-burly of the playground. The boy sprawls out on the floor with a book about trains. He reads with confidence and precision, isolating and testing syllables, piecing them methodically together into words. He is working fluently through some sentences about a station when the headmistress casually asks him what the word means. Being the boy he is, he works back logically from the words he has already read. The house where the engine driver lives? The place the trains rest when they're not running?

They were intelligent, and by any criteria, 'correct' answers. But the most common meaning of the word was beyond even his shrewd reasoning powers. In spite of living in an area of south London with perhaps the highest density of passenger services in the country, he had never travelled on a train or visited a station. The only trains he had ever seen were moving, not stopping. In books they always carried unfamiliar people that seemed to bear little resemblance to anyone he knew; how they got in the carriages in the first place was hardly his business. The notion that the likes of him and his family could have access to these vehicles – and consequently that places were provided where this could take place – was too far removed from his own experience ever to have occurred to him.

The first duty of any formal primary education must be to extend the child's range of experiences: to expose him to unfamiliar places and extraordinary people, and to sharpen his perception of those experiences he is *already* exposed to. The first of these aims is increasingly being met with 'the real thing'. Eight-year-olds go on camping holidays in forests, gaze down microscopes at living human tissue, and are talked to by local celebrities. But there are obvious limits to this, both economic and practical, and this is where the media are invaluable. Not many primary children will ever go on a school trip to Antarctica, or be allowed in the viewing gallery of an operating theatre. But on film and tape and disc they can share other people's experience of these things. They are vicarious experiences to be sure, but the young child's capacity for empathy is enormous, and the increasing technical refinements of many of the media make such experience something more than simply second-hand. No human eye has even seen *first*-hand the sights shown in that ravishing film made with a nylon filament lens inside working human organs. Nor is it possible for the human ear to hear fish noises unaided – and what primary-school child could resist a record of a haddock purring?

The list of similar examples of technological advances opening up previously hidden sights and sounds is growing all the time. Amongst the materials of an increasing number of primary schools you will now find examples of X-ray, micro- and infra-red photography. There may be films of dune-formation in deserts and life in city slums, or tapes of African hunting songs. Even the humble textbook illustration has vastly expanded its scope. Illustration was always rather a constricting notion, implying as it did the simple repetition in another medium of information already given in the text. In strictly factual books illustration of this sort is usually necessary if clarity is to be achieved. But in books which have hopes of stimulating the imagination as well it is often redundant if not downright dull. At its worst it can fix the fanciful meanderings which the text may have sparked off, on to some mundane, specific image. The trend in modern illustrated books is increasingly towards treating the pictures as statements in their own right, not as ancillaries to, or decorations of, the text. With the help of photographic libraries, new colour printing techniques and large page areas, the results can be very dramatic.

In the field of diagrams there have been advances

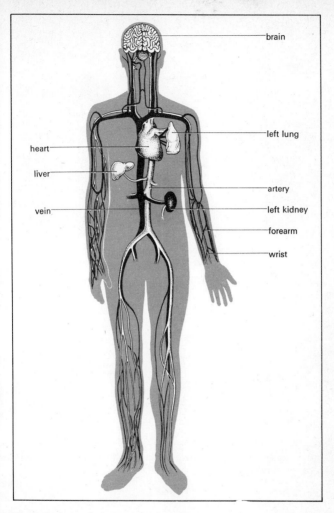

brain

left lung

heart

liver

artery

vein

left kidney

forearm

wrist

18. A diagram of a sort now common in textbooks, showing the clarity that can be achieved, even in black and white, with the skilful use of shading and airbrushing.

19. The rewards of technology. A high-speed photograph that could be a spur to imaginative writing and art just as much as a piece of scientific evidence.

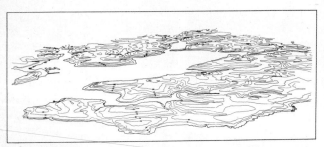

20. A topographical perspective produced by the Illustromat from a conventional map.

comparable to those brought about by animation and micro-photography in the motion-picture industry: the use of a single second colour for emphasis in an otherwise black and white picture, cut-away diagrams, and the use of over-laid transparent pages which can fold back layers of a mechanism or organism as succinctly as any dissection. The latest advance in the making of diagrams is the Illustromat, a computer-assisted drawing machine which can produce perspective views from plan drawings.

But television in the home probably remains the most powerful agent for extending the child's experience. Let no one be under any delusion about the degree to which primary children watch adult TV. As early as 1956 forty per cent of the ten to eleven age groups were watching television up till about a quarter to ten.[1] Today this would enable them to catch *Coronation Street*, *World in Action*, and most of *Play for Today*.[2] This book isn't really the place to discuss the quality of individual programmes, but there's little doubt that their incidental content[3] – speech patterns, gestures, expressions, styles of interaction between people, environments – can usefully extend the child's experience and powers of communication.

I once sat in on a junior class who were doing group

1. See *Television and the Child*, Hilde Himmelweit, Oxford, 1958.
2. The time the TV channels now unofficially assume that young children are in bed seems to be about 10.30 p.m.
3. Dealing with that other incidental content, the pervading life-style offered by television, is a more serious matter. But the problems it raises will never be solved by looking at television as some contagion which it is the school's duty to stamp out. The main hope here is that children will continue along the path they seem already set on, of assimilating television as a natural part of their world, taking it or leaving it alone as they please, learning to participate on both sides of the camera as their parents did with their box Brownies. This would seem to be a sounder basis for developing a healthily sceptical attitude towards the medium than the hysterical rejection which has constituted some adults' response.

improvisation round the theme of slums. The school was in a prosperous home-counties housing estate, but there were overspill children from London and the North, and the subject was no stranger to them. Yet there was not much acting out to be seen in their five-minute plays, no rows of children lying shoulder to shoulder on simulated beds. Indeed, most of the indoor scenes were delightfully whimsical, with the unemployed dad knocking up home-made furniture from the forest timber providentially growing near by. What, without exception, seemed to really fascinate these children was the confrontation with the landlord: the arrival of the rent collector, the tearful doorstep interrogations, the ritual of eviction and, for some unlucky families, prison.

With the gentlest of encouragement from the teacher, the idea grew that, though it made a fittingly dramatic conclusion, throwing a mother of seven summarily into clink was a little less than fair. So a trial was suggested, the idea needing little pushing since the children recognized a courtroom as being just as good for a slice of the action as an eviction. Their knowledge of courtroom procedure was remarkable, even though most of it had come undiluted from *Perry Mason*. All the children in the class clamoured to repeat the oath, and most could do it, bar the odd word.

Sadly, there was no time to explore beyond the clichéd posturings of TV trials into notions like the nature of evidence. But the children's knowledge of the broad outline of this particular way adults sort out their crises wasn't entirely valueless. They understood the need for an impartial judge and appreciated the right of an accused party to speak out in his defence. Most of all they had a strong sense of justice and mercy: the erring mum, I'm happy to report, was reprieved and found a job with the local council by a sympathetic court official!

A headmistress with long experience in one of the toughest areas of London's dockland, is convinced that 'the telly' can have a very beneficial effect on young children:

The primary age is the one where telly language 'takes'. If we do a piece of creative work in which everybody is involved – and it is usually just spoken language so that no one is at a disadvantage – what comes out, such as a play for voices, is a concoction of their organic Deptford language, which we haven't tried to obliterate, and Eliot and Orwell and the TV commercials and *Softly, Softly* and Dylan Thomas.

I do make a definite effort to cash in on anything that's been on the box. That is why I have a TV book tree. Surprisingly enough our children aren't always tuned into the same channel. I have found that our children dominate the television more than people would have you think. I think it is partly because they're on their own in the flat until latish at night. And they are very prepared to switch channels if they know there is something else on.

They will sit and listen to David Kossoff or Peter Ustinov just sitting in a chair, because it is this business of 'Brothers, here's a tale. Good, let it come.' They will always listen to a tale because it helps them escape into fantasy.

I have a feeling that children do not put out a hand spontaneously to take books unless a chord in them has already been touched. I have tried putting new books on display – and been careful not to put out single copies. I have put out six brand new

21. The magic of story-telling. It can captivate children as much on the television as in the flesh.

copies of each title. Some have been traditional tales, some have been about characters they have seen on TV, and some have been very new titles about modern subjects like space. The hands went out always to that which they had had some touch of before. TV came first, but the traditional story was chosen, even by boys, in preference to absolutely contemporary topics.[1]

Television has done little to disrupt children's traditional allegiances. It has thrown up a few cults, but they have been short-lived for the most part, like the fad for mid-Atlantic space-age puppets – which was quickly killed off by the appearance on the scene of real-life space-age puppets. TV has certainly given children greater access to these heroes and giants of the adult world, in all their dubious variety. But it hardly created the fascination, which has been there since before the time children began collecting cigarette cards of their favourite gangsters.

Whatever its other faults, television has not been a ve-hicle for some sort of technological brain-washing. At its best it has simply expanded the universe inside which chil-dren dream and play. Even at its worst, it may not be with-out educational merits, particularly in language develop-ment. Most language is learned by imitation, and as Paul Goodman has pointed out, unprompted imitation is the natural mode of learning outside formal institutions:

To be educated well or badly, to learn by a long process how to cope with the physical environment and the culture of one's society, is part of the human condition. In every society the edu-cation of the children is of the first importance. But in all societies, both primitive and highly civilized, until quite recently most education of most children has occurred incidentally. Adults do their work and other social tasks; children are not excluded, are paid attention to, and learn to be in-cluded. The children are not 'taught'. . . . Reality is often com-plex, but the young can take it by their own handle, at their

1. In conversation with the author.

own times, according to their own interests and initiative. Most important, they can imitate, identify, be approved or disapproved, co-operate and compete; there is socialization with less resentment, fear, or submission. The archetype of successful education is infants learning to speak, a formidable intellectual achievement that is universally accomplished. We do not know how it is done, but the main conditions seem to be what we have been describing: adult activity is going on, involving speaking; the infants are only incidental yet they participate, are attended to and spoken to; they play freely with their speech sounds; it is advantageous to them to make themselves understood.[1]

The relevance of this to children's relationship with the media is striking. The children who enacted that trial, pastiche though it may have been, might not have been able to deal with the quite sophisticated concepts involved without being prompted into the use of a 'special' language by the formal context of the trial. The educational sociologist, Basil Bernstein's, theory that working-class and middle-class children use different language 'codes' is becoming increasingly well known. He has suggested – and his suggestion has been readily agreed with by most working teachers – that working-class language tends to be fixed in the present, in specific contexts and concrete examples. Middle-class language tends to be more future-directed, generalized and abstract. Unfortunately, Bernstein's use of the phrase 'restricted' to describe the working-class style has led some readers to the assumption that he also meant that the language of working-class children was deprived and impoverished, that they actually *lacked*, as they might a chromosome, the crucial elements of middle-class language. Professor Bernstein's view on this is in fact very different:

Let us take [an] example. One mother when she controls her

1. 'The Present Moment in Education', Paul Goodman, *New York Review of Books*, 10 April 1969.

child places a great emphasis upon language because she wishes to make explicit and to elaborate for the child certain rules and the reasons for the rules and their consequences. In this way the child has access through language to the relationship between his particular act which evoked the mother's control and certain general principles and reasons and consequences which serve to universalize the particular act. Another mother places less emphasis upon language when she controls her child and deals with only the particular act and does not relate it to general principles and their reasoned basis and consequences. Both children learn that there is something they are supposed, or not supposed, to do, but the first child has learned rather more than this. The grounds of the mother's acts have been made explicit and elaborated whereas the grounds of the second mother's acts are implicit, they are unspoken. Our research shows just this: that the social classes differ in terms of the *contexts* which evoke certain linguistic realizations . . .

Because a code is restricted it does not mean that a child is non-verbal, nor is he, in the technical sense, linguistically deprived, for he possesses the same tacit understanding of the linguistic rule system as any child. It simply means that there is a restriction on the *contexts* and on the *conditions* which will orient that child to universalistic orders of meaning and to making those linguistic choices through which such meanings are realized and so made public. It does not mean that the children cannot produce at any time elaborated speech in particular contexts.[1]

One thing that can be said in favour of the media is that they dramatically expand the range of language styles and language-use contexts available to the child. Between the Bash Street Kids and *The Saint* and Oscar Wilde's short stories there are a lot of speech variants! The child retains most of them, and can potentially manipulate them all. It merely needs a sensitively chosen trigger situation to call them into play. So the learning frameworks which are cre-

1. 'A Critique of the Concept of "Compensatory Education" ', Basil Bernstein, in *Education for Democracy*, ed. Rubinstein and Stoneman, Penguin Books, 1970.

ated for the child – one of whose functions is to 'universalize' linguistic skills which may be tied to particular situations – must take the whole range of the child's language experience into account. Making use of their indigenous 'organic language' can, as every English teacher knows, bring out rich, imaginative material on their private lives. Recapping situations they have experienced in the media can similarly switch on whole areas of language which they have previously associated only with other people's speech. What invariably switches nothing on is the monologue – be it from teacher or book – that is couched in terms of the meanings and symbols of the literate and the middle class: an alien code delivered through alien channels.

There is no artifice in making deliberate use of the children's media experience in this way. If nothing else it is an effective technique. But it is also a gesture of respect for their way of life outside the school walls; it is not only teachers who are the bringers to the learning situation. And finally, episodes like that trial are the way children learn anyway in play: being 'another person', aping and parodying adult behaviour.

So far I have been speaking only of adult television. In what ways can specifically educational TV help extend young children's experience?

The most significant technical development here is closed-circuit TV (CCTV). This is simply a system in which signals are transmitted between camera and receiver by wire, rather than being broadcast. It is a system which is quite free of the restrictions on wave-bands and rigid scheduling which plague national broadcast television. And in the absence of any need for elaborate transmitters or heavy power sources even its technical operation is comparatively simple. Both these advantages have meant that control over CCTV can be left very much in the hands of working

The 'Mini-Studio'

Key

a) Close-up platform above projection box
b) Small top mirror
c) Slide projector
d) Film projector
e) Controls
f) Teacher's monitor
g) Operator's monitor
h) Underneath mirror and writing frame

1 & 2: Cameras

Scale

|___1___2 feet

22. Diagram of the sort of studio set-up suitable for intimate teacher operation in a small CCTV studio.

teachers. Programmes can be tailor-made for very small audiences and be delivered personally to them, down a wire. No 'air-time' is being used up, no other audiences edged out.

The merits of CCTV can be seen most clearly when the system is reduced to its basic essentials: a single teacher operating a light-weight camera and a large screen receiver in front of her own class. With mirrors and good lighting she can show her children detailed action in close-up that they would have difficulty in making sense of at a distance. It might be dissection, handwriting, crystal formation, or the fine details of a map. The teacher retains her flexible, first-hand contact with the children, and can use the camera when and how she thinks appropriate.

The same sorts of advantages are apparent when we consider net-worked CCTV. This is usually run by a local education authority and linked by land-line with the schools in its own area. There can be great flexibility of programming with this sort of arrangement. Many local stations have an abundance of channels, and run repeats just as often as the capacity of their recording equipment will allow. Again, the system scores heavily in the intimate portrayal of experiments and processes, and can often afford special demonstration equipment that would be beyond the budget of a single school.

But net-worked CCTV often assimilates the teacher as part of the process being televised, and here we begin to see its disadvantages. Inside a classroom, the teacher/producer has face-to-face contact with the children, and continuous feedback from them. The pace, level and direction of the demonstration and commentary can be continuously modified in the light of the way the children are reacting. But inside a studio, the teacher is forced to be a lecturer, and to present the material as it has been prepared in advance (unless the transmission is being distributed from inside *one* classroom to a large number of others).

When CCTV goes beyond this model, as it often does, and transmits drama and film then it is behaving in essentially the same way as broadcast educational television – Schools Television. And by the same measure Schools TV is often indistinguishable from 'adult'.

But the bulk of Schools Television broadcasts fall into the category of the illustrated lecture. They revolve around a presenter, who chats, introduces snippets of film, does experiments and talks to guest experts. I'd like to chart in detail the progress of one such programme – on the function of bones in the human body – since it usefully illustrates the typical virtues and defects of educational television.

The programme began with clear working models of joints and a studio demonstration by a young man, naked above the waist, of how the movements of these joints appeared in terms of limb and muscle movement. Then a collage of film clips of weight-lifters, sprinters, canoers and tennis players showing the variety of joint movements of which the body was capable. So far, so good. There followed an embarrassingly patronizing interlude, in which a puppet skeleton sang a jingle about the food that helps build bones, that was quite out of tune with the straight-talking and intelligent science that had gone before. The programme concluded with a specially filmed and hammily acted episode, following the progress of a boy who had fractured his arm.

So, doing a profit and loss account on this programme, what do we have? On the credit side, an intelligently selected and well-edited group of film clips that were as rich visually as they were helpful scientifically. Some concise demonstration (none of which however was beyond the capabilities of an enterprising class teacher). To be generous I would also include the presenter on the credit side, on the grounds of inoffensiveness, though for my taste his enthusiasm was too artificially wide-eyed and chummy.

On the debit side we have a drastic failure of tone in the puppet interlude, which was guilty, in terms of the level of the rest of the programme, of that worst of educational sins, talking-down. Any teacher working face-to-face with children would have avoided this mistake. And finally a piece of specially made film that most visually literate children, comparing it with the standards of the programmes they watch at home, would instantly reject as sloppy and unprofessional.

I do not want to be too hard on programmes of this type. They can be enormously useful as spring-boards, and can assemble a wide range of useful material that would take a teacher weeks to prepare. And we must not forget that the switched-on set still has a capacity to hold children's attention even if the programmes themselves are turned off.

In general, if we look at the advantages of educational television, at the characteristics which make best use of the medium's potentialities and give a service which teachers could not reasonably expect from any other source, we are reduced to three: readily and cheaply available film, accessibility to articulate and witty lecturers, and clear demonstrations of elaborate processes and experiments. These constitute a valuable and formidable contribution. But it would be as well to remember the comparatively low educational value of the second, and how much better the third is served by materials which can be stopped, slowed down and repeated at will (of which more later). Broadcast TV is, too, a didactic medium. It speaks out, and the whole class – teacher included – must attend together. They cannot talk back at the programme or ponder on what is being shown. They must assimilate at the same rate as the set disgorges. Their only course if they wish to explore an idea while it is still fresh is to switch off.

It's illuminating to compare the type of programme I described above with the American series *Sesame Street*.[1] I know that in some ways this is an unfair comparison; *Sesame Street* has enormous financial backing not only from the government, but from a host of private foundations. But I think that this is more than balanced by the narrowness of the educational brief it has to work to. There is no

1. Before this book is published a selection of *Sesame Street* programmes will have been shown in Britain on ITV.

23. Filming skywriting for a *Sesame Street* sequence on the letter D. Apart from their inherent interest, devices like this show the constancy of letters, regardless of their shape and size.

24. Oscar. the gloomy resident of the Street's trashcan.

concession in *Sesame Street* to the unpredictable, open-ended world of ideas and imagination upon which the best of British primary teaching is based. It is a crash rehabilitation programme for the educationally deprived, with no other aim than to develop their basic vocabulary and counting skills.

But the manner in which it has elected to do this defies categorization in terms of what we understand as educational television. It is exhaustive in treatment (each programme is nearly one hour long), fast-moving and sophisticated. In spite of the infantile level of much of its intellectual content, its tone and style are forthright and unpatronizing. It doesn't assume that just because children are unable to write the only speech they can accept is baby-talk. As well as this respect for its viewers as people, it has a very high estimate of the standards they expect from the media. The graphics, animation and music would all do credit to a film festival entry. And the programmes are peppered with references to the *Andy Williams Show*, the latest soul records, and so on.

Some typical sequences would show letter shapes being formed by sky-writing planes; a specially-made five-minute action film (plus folk-song to match) naming the parts of the body; racy sequences about specific numbers, which cut from multicoloured animations of the figure, like the count-down before a pop show, to filmed cameo jokes of the number in question manifest, for instance, as a festoon of cameras around a photographer's neck.

The programme makes great use of delightfully bizarre creatures and animals in the Dr Seuss mould. Most of them are endearingly slow-witted (except for the blasé and donnish Kermit, the frog) or have some other difficulty in communicating. And it is this that is one of the programme's strokes of genius. Two plodding labourers try and share out evenly an uneven number of jelly beans, until one sneakily abolishes the problem by eating one. A mute dog desperately tries to order a paper from a news-stand – and at every stage the newsman flunks his reading of the dog's mime. By this time you know that the kids watching will be jumping up in their seats and screaming the right answers. It is the old pantomime trick of the deliberate mistake, the dramatic irony, the misunderstanding dragged out so maddeningly that the children in the audience cannot contain themselves any longer. It was a masterly stroke to adapt this technique for television, and so *guarantee* the involvement of viewers in what is, after all, one of the least directly involving media. And all the while, in sketches of this sort with 'dumb birds' and mute dogs, there is a constant undertone of respect and understanding for those who have language difficulties.[1]

Sesame Street probably sets its sights unnecessarily low. But for all that it is a model of how to make full use of the potentialities of a medium. It also makes very clear that educational television ignores at its peril the experience which the children have had of the media outside school.

I must bring this discussion back more closely to the theme of experience. The one type of learning experience that *only* broadcast television can give – the sense of *now* – is precisely the one that has been almost totally neglected. In spite of the conspicuous successes of live outside broadcast TV, and the way it 'fits' the medium, I know of no attempts to extend this approach into the educational field. Yet the potentialities are enormous: live broadcasts from

1. It is curious the effect which talking animals have on children. Some research workers in Britain have made striking progress with children with severe speech difficulties, by implanting small loudspeakers and microphones inside their favourite toy animals. The teacher sits, unseen, in a separate room, and carries on a dialogue with the child, using the toy as a mouthpiece.

25. A classic *Sesame Street* tactic. The two clowns are so exasperatingly inept in their approach to the problem of how to change the bulb that the children watching will work out the logical solution before them.

26. A scene from a BBC TV film of a potholing expedition, that would have been doubly riveting broadcast live. Or would the possibility of an accident make this too risky a prospect with a young audience?

archaeological digs (not recorded like the BBC's ambitious series from Cadbury), dispatches from expeditions and surveys, even programmes from research laboratories. Of course, it could be argued that such programmes would inevitably contain long stretches when nothing of great interest was on the screen, or unpredictable flashes when, for safety's and decency's sake, there was too much. But why is it not education's business to cope with the protracted and the unexpected? In any case, children respond so positively to the feel of authenticity that comes across from live television that it could be of some value used to show nothing more than the safe workings of a typing pool.

Videotape recording will help eliminate many of the drawbacks associated with broadcast educational TV. Just as a radio programme can be recorded onto magnetic tape, so television sound and visuals can be recorded onto electronic videotape. The tape can be played back through the videotape recorder on which it was made, and shown on an ordinary television receiver. The apparatus is simple enough for both children and teachers to use, and is getting cheaper all the time. The TV recorder costs about £400, and each tape about £15. Both BBC and ITV have now removed most of the copyright obstacles to the recording and replaying of their educational programmes by schools. (They are also discussing the idea of an educational licence fee, payable by local authorities in return for more freedom to use recorded TV material, wider access to archives, and perhaps a regular delivery service of pre-recorded, topical videotapes.)

So we are entering a situation where a teacher can pre-record a programme, view it at his leisure, prepare a teaching programme to go with it, show it at the time he thinks it will be most useful, stop it at any point he pleases and replay it an almost unlimited number of times.

Videotape seems to answer perfectly almost all the worries I expressed above about broadcast TV for schools. Yet even it has its drawbacks. It is, firstly, heavily teacher controlled. Unless it is used as a sort of visual note-taker by a class watching the original broadcast, the teacher makes the decision about what programmes to record, alone and remote from the classroom situation. Secondly, the price of videotape means that there is a limit to the number of programmes a school can store. Either they are irrevocably deleted to make room for new material, or the option of recording future programmes is surrendered. So videotape

27. An electronic video recording set in operation in a junior classroom. A single cassette can give up to sixty minutes of sound and pictures. There is no need to blackout, no disturbing projector noise. The teacher can watch the children react, and if she wants, talk over the sound track.

recording does not really meet two important criteria of a good primary learning situation: access for the *child* to the teaching materials, and some sort of permanence about these materials so that they can reasonably be looked on as reference sources.

But the latest development in television technology, electronic video recording, may well turn out to be the most revolutionary influence on visual education. The technology is very complicated, but its result is that the sound and visuals from either film or videotape can, by a combination of optical and electronic recording, be stored either on disc or on film in a compact cassette. This can then be played back, like a sound disc or cassette, through an ordinary television set to which an adaptor has been fitted. Like videotape the cassettes can be stopped at any point, rewound

74

and played back. Unlike videotape they can be mass produced, and are cheap, compact and resilient enough to be regarded as library items, rather than temporary records.

If all the promises which have been made about it come true, electronic video recording could do for moving picture communication what the paperback did for the written word. One of the greatest handicaps the television and the cinema industries have laboured under is the enormously expensive and complicated paraphernalia needed for their continued operation. Centralization and economies of scale were regrettably inevitable; giant studios, oligopolistic production and distribution combines – even the picture house itself, the mass viewing theatre. What is offered to the public through these media is conceived for massive audiences and shown to massive audiences – simultaneously, and at the time most convenient for the manufacturer. Any programme which does not quite fit into this monolithic system, for instance a film for a minority audience which is only free to watch during peak viewing hours, stands little chance of being made.

Electronic video recording, which means that you can buy, store and play the moving pictures you want, when you want, through a gadget that is now more common in homes than a bathroom, utterly destroys the basis for the old pattern. Even the moguls may soon be able to look at eccentric minority audiences without contempt. But the great hope, if all the considerable legal copyright problems can be overcome, is that a host of small production companies will come into existence and begin to produce film cassettes for primary school gerbil keepers, stamp collectors, Egyptologists, medieval music revivalists, antique-car enthusiasts, and all the other *real* minority audiences.

None of this will happen quickly. The discs and cassettes will be expensive initially and will emerge from something

75

analogous to a paperback publishing operation, that is, the mass copying of films and programmes already in existence. But, all being well, a 'hardback' situation, with smaller runs of specially produced materials, will quickly follow. Either way it will be a momentous day for the primary school when any child can set up and show himself films like David Cobham's version of T. H. White's *The Goshawk*, or *The Tribe that Hides from Man*.

First-Hand

School visits to field centres, art galleries, museums, etc. are not really inside the scope of this book; but I talked earlier about 'sense experience' and I think it is relevant to mention the materials which the latter are sending to the schools. Many museums now run extensive school services, not only mounting exhibitions but employing freelance craftsmen to make replicas and models for distribution to schools. A primary school in an area serviced by a good museum can probably borrow for a few weeks anything from a stuffed heron to a perfect working model of a vertical

28. A working model of a siege catapult distributed to primary schools by the Museum Schools Service.

steam engine. But even these services admit that there is no substitute for the real thing. They are trying wherever possible to get the exhibits out of the glass cases, and back into use – or at least back into the hand. Give one child a medieval sandal, and another an almost indistinguishable twentieth-century replica, and there is no comparison between the creative work they produce. Like live television an original object carries a powerful charge of authenticity for a child. It has been handled, worn, discussed, and thrown away by real people. It has lived through invasions, wars, excavations. It has *mana*, and by this the young child is entranced.[1]

The enlargement of the child's purely sensory experience is greatly helped by these objects distributed by museums. He can feel the texture of rocks and minerals, smell fur, and get a sense of the scale of the environment in which people of earlier times lived. But there are other agents of sense education which, because of their special and intimate relationship with the media, I think I should also mention here. These are the works of the front-runners in *avant-garde* art and music. There are many who have little time for the products of this movement, which they see as riddled with contradictions and hypocrisy. How can silence be music, or humdrum commercial packaging be presented as sculpture? The worship of chance, the absence of any human dimension, the deliberate refusal by the artist to make any statement through his work, are at complete variance with our traditional notions of what art is about. But maybe all that is wrong is that these creations, with the connivance of their manufacturers (who nevertheless appear to despise the word) came to be called 'art', when

1. And the adult too, to judge by the crowds who gathered to gaze at the totally undistinguished sample of moon-dust brought back by Apollo 11.

29. A giant inflatable structure in which children can for a while defy all the rules which adults make for their safety. It's undeniably a magnificent monster toy; yet its smaller cousins can be regularly seen in modern art galleries.

they are really something different. For young children can see very well their value. They are *fun*. Not many primary kids would fail to see the joke in Andy Warhol's blown-up Campbell soup tins, and I doubt if any at all could resist Claes Oldenburg's giant foam-rubber hamburger. This is the world of play and testing, an exploration not so much of human relationships, as of things and materials, and the potentialities of one's own body. To the extent to which this heightens the perceptive powers of all the senses it is also not without human importance.

Primary children have anticipated virtually every *avant-garde* style: Dadaist collages, action painting, kinetic sculpture. Today, working with materials which relate to the subject either sympathetically or incongruously is an almost obligatory feature of primary school art. So you will find nuts glued into squirrel friezes, and decidedly solid elephants put together out of disposable egg-boxes. And I wonder how many of the music teachers who find John Cage's 'compositions' for silent piano arrogant and nonsensical have ever asked their classes to stay perfectly quiet for a few minutes and just listen to what is happening around them?

30. Egg boxes: to the primary child, instant reptilian skin.

Personalized Instruction and Self-Education

One thing that almost all primary teachers agree about is the virtue of helping children learn individually. They may argue about whether the direction of this learning should be in the hands of the child or the school, and to what degree the learning should be punctuated by teaching. But few will dispute that, bright or dull, destined to support the old order or create a new, all children are *different*, and no one will benefit if they are treated as the same.

Some teachers would go further and say that a child should not only have a bespoke curriculum, but do much of the measuring and tailoring himself. They would argue that no teacher can ever wholly understand a child's interests and capabilities, or predict that remote, improbable topic which will fire intellect and imagination, like falconry did with Billy in *Kes*. Guide a child down a curriculum – however rich and unorthodox – that *you* have designed for him, and where what he retains is superficial and irrelevant, and you run the risk of bypassing areas where an explosion of genuine learning and growth could take place.

79

Either way, the media have an important role to play both in personalized instruction and self-education. For a start, no teacher can ever have the time to give round-the-clock individual attention to thirty-plus children; nor, with the greatest respect, is she likely to have the intellectual resources to do such a job. She is a teacher after all, not a Leonardo.

Now, the media's flexibility and motivating power, the way they focus other teaching talents into the classroom, above all the ease with which they can be used by a single child working at his own rate, make them invaluable for work developing in this way. Their products can be pieced together by the teacher into tightly-structured packages, or lumped together with the hardware into a giant hoard of equipment and materials through which the child can meander as he wishes. In this section I'm going to look at the ways in which some of the media can help the child working by, or for, himself.

The Word

In some ways radio is an ideal auto-instructional aid. It can be authoritative, realistically 'live', and capture the authentic, precise flavour of a personality talking better even than television. Yet – operating in a single dimension, aerated with silences and the flexible rhythms of microphone speech, it actively involves the listener like few other media. That single thread of sound is all he is given. The time, the place, the faces are his to fashion as he will. Any teacher who has used a skilfully told radio story or historical reconstruction will know just what remarkable fantasies the children can weave around them.

Here is an extract from a BBC Schools Radio Broadcast on the initiation rites of some young Bushman boys in the

Kalahari desert. It is in that classic radio mode: 'as if you were there':

The sand in this clearing looks as if it's been trampled, and there are the ashes of old fires. Gai and Samgau look round nervously, but in fact nothing's going to happen for a day or two. They'll have a fire, and a shell of water, but hardly any food, just a few beans to chew perhaps. For two or three days they've got to stay here alone and *starve*. It sounds hard, but the bushmen say it will put them in the right frame of mind, and all hunters have to learn how to bear hunger and thirst. Altogether Gai and Samgau will spend four weeks in this place. Let's run the days together and go forward in time to a week from now . . .

Gai and Samgau are dancing. They and the older men have been dancing for a day and night. They dance and rest in turn. Look, poor Gai stumbles and nearly falls. His father doesn't help him, and Gai goes on dancing. Samgau is covered with sweat and dust. His mouth is open and his eyes are staring and his legs seem to move automatically. Gai watches him. Samgau needed some discipline. Suddenly Samgau cries out and falls on the ground. Gai drags him away from the fire. He looks satisfied. Samgau could become a medicine man, a healer, then he would dance at the curing dances, challenge the great gods, pull the evil out of people and throw it away into the desert. Gai is still dancing. Oh, he makes a false step and his father stops him – and corrects him. Gai goes on dancing – and on, and on . . .

Another week has passed and Gai and Samgau are sitting round the fire with their fathers. They're learning a hunting chant. Samgau holds up his hand. The men listen approvingly: Look, these are my hands/ I shoot with my hands/ With my arrows I shoot them/ I kill meat with my hands/ So that we eat meat/ Give us meat . . .

The last week. Gai and Samgau have been hunting again, and Gai has a buck and Samgau has one of the great elands. What days and days of exhausting tracking of the beasts across the desert have led up to this. And now there's one more ordeal. The animals are butchered and scraps are burned in the fire. Gai and Samgau squat in front of their fathers. Their foreheads are cut with the animals' horns, and the burnt scraps rubbed into the wounds. Sweat and blood run down, but Gai and Samgau don't make a sound. Now, they have the animals' strength and eyesight and watchfulness. Now, at last, they are hunters . . .

from *Children of the Bush*, written by Margery Morris, BBC
Radio 4, 19 February 1971.

The reading was sensitive without being theatrical, and
'atmosphere' was provided by authentic Bushman music
and speech. This particular programme could clearly be
commended on grounds of vividness and anthropological
respectability alone. But what I found most interesting was
its honest handling of the more unsettling scenes, and the
way this was related to the characteristics of radio as a
medium. The same absence of exhaustive detailing that
makes radio as stimulating to a child's imagination as to his
intellect, helped this programme to present the boys as *children*, not as creatures of some alien species. There was a
sense of the 'otherness' of Bushman culture without any
feeling that this separated them from us. On television there
could be no avoiding the strangeness of those faces; on
radio, Gai and Samgau could well be cousins of the immi-
grant children in the next desks. The inevitable gaps in
radio's crayoning-in of any subject give the listener room to
relate that subject to features of his life he can already cope
with.

Other types of radio programme have been successful by
copying well-known entertainment models. The BBC's
Music Club, for instance, is based on the 'sound magazine'
formula. There are resident 'personalities' that the children
come to know and look forward to as the series progresses,
a marvellous range of materials, from medieval songs to
talks on how to make your own *musique concrète* with
vacuum cleaners and edited tape; invitations to the children
to participate in the programme by sending in tapes and
ideas; and above all a nice irreverence of tone (and often of
content) that makes the children feel the programme is on
their side.

There are some technical drawbacks to the classroom use of radio, but most of these can now be overcome. A child wishing to listen by himself without disturbing the rest of the class can use a miniature earphone. The teacher wishing to repeat a broadcast, or use one which was put out at an inconvenient time, can tape-record it. This has been permitted by the BBC (provided certain conditions are met) for considerably longer than the recording of television broadcasts. Indeed, the Corporation itself has capitalized on this provision by devising a system called Radiovision which consists basically of a set of slides planned for use with a tape-recorded version of a broadcast programme. It is an admirably cheap, do-it-yourself version of the professional lantern lecture. This system is most useful in contexts where the illustrated lecture is likely to be of value; that is, where a specific set of ideas and images need to be conveyed to the children. Like bad text-book illustrations, a clumsy use of pictures with a radio programme can stifle the children's personal interpretations of those ambiguous, Penny Plain sounds.

But if, being fanciful for a moment, radio is the *femme fatale* of self-educational media – elusive, seductive, a weaver of dreams – it is the book which is the most flexible, solid, all-purpose workhorse. It has become customary to apologize for this, as if the continued thriving of this two-thousand-year-old device was an affront to the Electronic Age. This is about as short-sighted as lamenting the survival of family doctoring in an age of heart-lung machines and intensive care units. The book is not just a supreme technological invention in its own right; it is a channel which can distil, integrate and present many of the advances in other media – just as the GP brings not a little modern cardiology along with his bedside manner.

A book has something of a bedside manner too. It is still

a more agreeable object to take between the sheets than a television set. It is portable and easy to work. It can fit snugly into a pocket – or at least a satchel. In most cases it is *yours*. That a book can be a personal possession is a crucial feature of its educational usefulness. Young children are very responsive to this quality, and quickly seek to impress their identity on any book that comes into their grasp. The previous owner's name is butchered, obliterated with a hundred inky scratches or preferably turned into some dirty word by the subtle changing of a few characters. Up goes the new copper plate: Smith, J., the School, Marlborough, Wiltshire, England, Europe, the World, the Universe. My own memory of book-doctoring is for some reason fixed on the Shorter Latin Primer, which we feebly changed to Shortbread Eating Primer. You can't develop that sort of intimacy with a film loop.

But the indignities which books have to suffer in school are symptoms of the ambivalent feelings which young children have about them. The traditional textbook – as an *educational* device – can only be looked on with hostility. It is the epitome of that other world of school, of boredom, stuffiness, discipline and grown-upness. Hence the guerrilla attacks on the book's pomposity, the changed words, the limericks in the back. But at the same time, books as objects are good to have around, especially the new ones that smell of ink and machines. You can snap them shut and search the pages for rude words. You may even browse voluntarily through the illustrations before you stack them away in the desk.

Of course, this is a picture which is rapidly becoming dated. Primary textbooks are improving and being treated more naturally as a result. But the paradox remains. On the one hand children like books as objects because they can *work* them. On the other, books can symbolize for many children that world of middle-class learning which they may feel has already abandoned them. (Indeed there are very few books which are not written in the language of that world.) It seems to me crucial that a way is found of resolving this paradox, for the unrealized potentialities of the text-book are enormous.

Consider for a moment some of the advantages which books have over other auto-instructional media. Portability I have already mentioned – though this will soon be shared by other media, as schools become more tolerant of children borrowing discs and slides for home use. Their ease of re-wind and playback, though, is never likely to be rivalled! But it is the book's passivity, its incapability of pressurizing the reader, that is its most valuable feature as an aid for personalized instruction and self-education. Books can be used at almost any level of concentration. They can be dipped into, skimmed or browsed through. The reader's speed automatically adjusts itself to the rate at which he can understand the text. (Though children at the younger end of the primary age range can sometimes regard reading as more of a technical exercise than anything connected with meaning. Which is why many teachers are understandably wary of reading schemes that try to teach phonetic reading expertise divorced from spoken language and real-life situations.) If the book is illustrated the child can link picture and text in almost any way he wishes – or choose to interpret them quite separately. There is nothing like the sort of insistent, organic link that exists between a film and its commentary.

In these ways books respect their readers. As a medium they can give their audience very great freedom of use and interpretation. But they possess other characteristics which can militate against this. The book's image is one of authoritativeness; it is where you go to 'find the facts' – or at least to check them. To a child its answer is final (unless it happens to be challenged by TV). This inflated status can have dangerous consequences. It discourages scepticism in the child. It excuses the hectoring tone in which so many school books are written (so easy to fall into when there is no one there by the typewriter to answer back).

There are certain types of book in which these tendencies are especially exaggerated. One is the non-fiction 'story' or fictional documentary, the attempt to ease children into some superficially dull (usually social studies) topic by writing a fictional narrative around it. I have before me four books[1] that graphically illustrate the weakness of this *genre,* the more so because they are so obviously well intentioned.

The books concern the march of progress in an imaginary rural county called Rilshire. In the tones of a well-mannered local newspaper they detail the transition of a traditional and predominantly agricultural environment into a modern industrial one. Farmland is buried beneath the motorways; old cottages give way to tower blocks; a branch railway line closes down and a New Town goes up. The books give proper space to the protest actions, and never omit a passing mention of those who are suffering as a result of the changes. But the end result is never in doubt. The fuddy-duddies are squashed and each book ends with the attainment of some small, bright Utopia. Neighbours chat happily as they walk across the traffic-free shopping precinct. The young, New Town executives park their Jaguars outside the open-plan plastics factory. Granny gazes down from her tower block at the children's play-space beneath. We never learn the fate of the beaten and the bewildered, whose lives have been changed in ways beyond their control; they are abandoned on earlier pages:

1. *The Changing Scene*, R. P. A. Edwards, Burke, 1970.

These older shopkeepers sold out and their shops were bought by younger, more progressive men. They, too, modernized and soon Rockton's shopping-centre took on a bright, chromium-plated look.

The old folk grumbled and said that the new-style shops were not homely, but most people were pleased with the changes.

All this did not happen over-night. The changes took a number of years and caused inconvenience and hardship to quite a lot of people.

This is not the place to argue over particular interpretations of 'progress'. My concern in this book is with the way certain modes of communication serve educational ends, and I fear that the choice of the fictional documentary form was the worst possible one for a subject of this sort.

Whatever one's own view of 'modernization' there can be little argument that the function of education is to make a critical, humanist evaluation of the concept. How much do 'old folk' and 'homeliness' matter? How do you measure 'hardship'? It cannot be education's business to persuade children to accept a certain course of events as inevitable. Yet it is precisely an overwhelming feeling of inevitability that pervades these books. Events march on as inexorably as the narrative. Stories have a beginning and an end, and so, therefore, must social change. The beginning is the old traditional market town; the proper end, the architect-planned suburb. Real life, needless to say, is not as tidy or clear-cut as this.

The form of these books excludes children from seeing the intricacies of change, and the part which humans can play in directing their lives. The fictional documentary, more than any other form, moves in a way that cannot involve young children. Not being proper fiction, it has no flesh and blood characters with which the children can identify and appreciate the real human dimensions of the changes. Yet not being proper 'fact' either it has no point of convincing engagement with their lives. Why not use real newspaper cuttings instead of fake ones? I know the dangers of over-particularizing events. But they are not as great as those of over-generalizing, of telling an abstract story so relentlessly that it seems that things could never happen any other way.

These books are an example of one sort of dogmatism to which the book as a medium is prone. There are others in the field of social attitudes. Stereotyping, prejudice and propaganda can be great problems in primary school books. They rarely come across with the emotional persuasiveness of film and television, but they have an insidious permanence. The book's authority can make its impact considerable, particularly at an age at which social attitudes are still fluid. Class bias, for instance, is very common. The children depicted in so many primary texts, running up their long garden to meet Daddy getting out of his Rover, have always been a joke. But racial bias is not so funny. The University of Sussex Centre for Multi-racial Studies did an analysis in 1969 of a number of the most popular reading schemes in use in infant school. It found no evidence of any outright prejudice, but a strong tendency to ignore non-Caucasian groups, or to talk about them as quaint savages,

31. Too many primary textbooks still seem trapped in a pre-war Arcadia where the children, bare-kneed and scrubbed, play for endless summer holidays in their country gardens.

and a persistent equation of white with good and black with bad.

This, then, is the paradox of the school text-book. The practice of reading is a comfortable and flexible one, admirably suited to learning situations where the child is in control, or at least being allowed to progress at his own rate. Yet the text-book itself can be both symbolically hostile and practically authoritarian. Is there anything we can learn from the way that books are used in primary schools which might help us to resolve these contradictions?

The one sure thing is that the days of the standard course book, handed out to every child in a class and prescribing in detail a year's work, are numbered. Almost every recent development in the pattern of primary work eliminates the need for books of this sort: the integration of subjects, the growth of project work by small groups and individual children, the desire to keep the syllabus sufficiently open to allow for responses to unexpected and topical situations. The curriculum inside this sort of educational set-up is more like a Meccano set than a finished machine. There is a battery of basic components which can be put together in any number of ways, broken down again into smaller units, and added to as the progress of the work throws up new goals and possibilities.

Written materials for children working in this way need to be of three basic types. Firstly, high quality imaginative literature – stories, poetry and the sort of stimulating scientific *belles lettres* of gifted scientists like Gilbert White and Darwin. Second, hardcore reference books, where children already deeply immersed in a subject can go for the gen. Finally, 'prompt' materials, whose function is to spark off interest in a child, provoke him into asking questions, suggest guidelines for work and experimentation and give him a skeleton of information on which to base this work.

89

The first type is a familiar object in all schools and its development in the future depends simply on a recognition of the breadth of material which can involve and excite the child. This is as likely to come from playground jingles and Japanese Haiku as from the *Golden Treasury*.

Reference books specially created for children are probably redundant, if not actually dangerous. At the stage at which a child really wants and needs to go to a reference book (and is there any point in him going at any other stage?) he will probably find a clear adult text the ideal answer. There is nothing more intellectually frustrating to a child who has reached this pitch of inquisitiveness, who has 'picked up the scent', than being fobbed off with diluted, out-of-date 'children's' books. So what is needed in this second region is a well-stocked library of authoritative yet comprehensible books (and if they are this, labels like adults' or children's become meaningless) to which the child has

32. For a child deep in a project, the material in hardcore reference books is perfectly assimilable. Indeed, he will rarely be satisfied by anything less.

the freest possible access. Primary schools which operate libraries on this principle, allowing children to record their own borrowings and returnings, find it works perfectly. The loss rate is never more than one or two per cent a year (and if the books have been pinched, it is probably for homes where they are needed).

It is the third type of written material, which I labelled the 'prompt' category, that presents most difficulties, but also, perhaps, the most exciting challenge. The most obvious solution is not a book at all but something approximating to a work-card. The Jackdaw-type pack of source sheets, photographs, documents and work-sheets is the ultimate expression of this idea. To a teacher, this is an attractive device. Superficially it is considerably more flexible than a book. It can be broken up into its individual components and dispersed amongst a group of children working on different aspects of a topic. And the teacher can fairly easily produce comparable packs from her own resources. (Indeed, conscientious teachers have always produced their own work-cards, sometimes to the extent of tailoring them for individual children.) For personalized assignment or experiment details, this style of presentation cannot be rivalled.

The Photographic Work Cards produced by John Copus and Barry Latter[1] are a good example. They are printed on stiff, resilient card, with a photograph on one side and a series of questions and projects which could be sparked off (and partly solved) by the photo on the other.

But I think it is only fair to look at the drawbacks of these cards as well. Consider, for instance, how they may appear to a child. They bear little resemblance to any of the media he is used to handling outside school. Physically they are set firmly on teacher's side of the fence. And as we are talking

1. Published by Longmans, 1971.

This wall is very cleverly built. There is no cement or mortar to bond the stones together, yet it will withstand animals pushing against it, all sorts of weather and even plants growing in it. It is made of Cotswold Stone (Oolitic Limestone) and is called a 'dry stone' wall.

1   sandstone, granite, chalk, kaolin, rock salt.
Find out all you can about these kinds of rock. Discover where they

33, 34. Two ideal work-cards. The subjects are self-contained without being insular. The photographs have been carefully chosen as springboards, one as clear visual evidence from which the children can actually work, the other as an evocative stimulus to imaginative writing and drama.

can be found in the British Isles, their uses and any other interesting information. Write about each one and illustrate your article with drawings. A book about geology will help.

2   Do you notice the uneven pattern made by the stones in the wall? Make your own 'wall' pattern on paper, like this:
Cover a piece of paper with wax crayon. Try to get some texture on your paper by putting it over a rough surface whilst you are crayoning, such as the floor or a brick wall. When you have finished, cut your paper into stone shapes, similar to those in the picture, and stick them on to black or white paper and build your own wall.

3   It was hard work to build this dry stone wall. Look at different types of walls in and around your school. Feel the stones or bricks. Imagine you were building the wall in the picture. How did you build such a wall? Imagine the problems you were faced with, who came along and gave good or bad advice. When it was finished, were you pleased with your work? Write all about it.

4   In this picture stone is used as a grindstone for sharpening tools such as scythes, sickles, choppers, billhooks, axes, mattocks, and pickaxes. Find out all you can about these and other large cutting tools, draw each one and describe its use.

5   Read one of these poems:
Mending Wall by Robert Frost
A Time to Talk by Robert Frost

Alley way

35.

36.

The alley way in the photograph is in a town. In Yorkshire and Lancashire an alley way is sometimes called a snicket or a ginnel.

1 This alley way would make a wonderful place in which to hide. Write a newspaper report about a person or an animal found hiding here. Make your report as exciting as possible.

2 It is mysterious and dark at the end of the alley. Where does it lead to? With some of your friends, make up a play or mime about some boys and girls who squeezed through the narrow passage at the end, found themselves in a different world and had an extraordinarily strange adventure.

3 Paint or make a picture of an alley way with cut out shapes from old magazines. Use a long, narrow piece of paper like the one on the left.

4 Find some plants growing in odd places round your school. e.g., plants between paving stones and on roofs. Describe the plants and where they were found. How do you imagine that they got there?

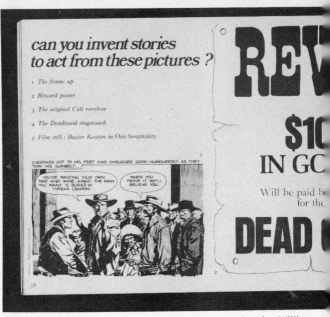

37. A spread from Evans's *Exploration Drama* series, by William Marting and Gordon Vallins. The magazine style, apart from making

of self-education in this section, it is as well to remember the difficulty which young children may have in making sense of a piece of completely context-free paper. Even the argument that this form is an ideal way of giving flavour to reproductions of historical documents is not a good one. We have already discussed how sensitive children are to authenticity. To them, a replica of a Victorian broadsheet is just a replica, whether it is a life-size photocopy of the original, or reset in Times Roman on a book page. The former may indeed be more interesting to them than the latter, but this is nothing to do with its 'authenticity' or its existence as a single sheet.

I am not trying to underrate the value of single sheet and

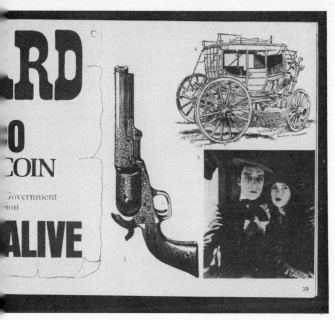

non-book-readers feel at home, can open up opportunities for new sorts of classroom activity.

work-card models. But they are not a medium which automatically solves every self-educational problem. (And as I shall discuss later, a more careful consideration of the different educational functions of sheets and books could help greatly towards the rationalization of the production of materials between teachers and publishers.)

The book, for all its superficial inflexibility and alien image, may have rather greater potentialities. All an aid needs to qualify for the category of 'book' is sheets of paper bound between covers. It doesn't need to resemble those arid tomes first published in the thirties ('twenty-nine impressions since'). It can look like a magazine, or a comic. It can have huge pages and be lavishly illustrated in colour. It can, above all, be made to look like the sort of printed material which the child feels is a part of *his* world.[1]

There is nothing necessarily vulgar about these forms. Indeed, they can more readily accommodate many currently desirable educational objectives than staider forms of written material. Magazines, for instance, are the archetype of the interdisciplinary aid. The juxtaposition of poetry and graphs, paintings and questionnaires, looks perfectly natural in this format. And this style of presentation can give the book a flexibility in use that is belied by its physical solidity. Being a book, linear and sequenced in structure, it can give a child working by himself some sort of order and context to the material he is examining. But there is no need for him to take any notice of this. If he wishes he can open the book at random and nibble at whatever takes his fancy. Nor is there any need for him to respond to the juxtapositions in the way the author may have intended. I suggested earlier that a book does not press the relationships between word and image in the way that a film does. This is one of the beneficial side-effects of reading being an *active* process: the deciphering of anything other than large print requires a fine and specific focusing of the eye. One word, one sentence must be examined at a time. You cannot, as you can with film or television, be forced to experience a number of ideas simultaneously.

There are other techniques by which books can be opened up to all sorts of readers working in all sorts of ways. Captions and headings can be put together at a vocabulary level simpler than that of the text proper, to provide a gateway for the poorer readers. And typographical and journalistic devices can considerably increase the impact of a book for a young reader. The use of treble

1. The Plowden report discovered that 29 per cent of all homes possessed less than six books.

columns, for instance (and consequently of very short lines of type), can make a book both livelier and easier to read.

The Schools Council linguistic development scheme for five-plus children, *Breakthrough to Literacy*, is perhaps the most ambitious scheme to embody many of the points I have been discussing. The 'Breakthrough' reading books that form an integral part of the scheme are bright, paperbound books, illustrated in the best commercial styles, and based around the stories, conversation and language structure of the children themselves.

The Light

The technological development which has done most to expand the potentialities of film as a self-educational medium has been nothing more than the ground glass screen. With the assistance of various systems of mirrors this has enabled films to be projected in a small space in daylight. The elaborate arrangements which previously accompanied the showing of even a ten-minute film meant that it was economically and organizationally unjustifiable unless a considerable number of children were watching simultaneously. A room with a blackout had to be booked in advance and a projectionist laid on. Since the room was in darkness during the showing of the film, no children could be engaged in any other activities. If the film was stopped for too long for the examination of a particular frame there was a good chance that it would melt. If it did, the sense of drama and occasion encouraged by the darkened room could mean that the whole class would collapse in chaos.

Now a child can sit at a table in a corner of a class in daylight and show himself a documentary film through a box of mirrors and screens which give a picture area something like a foot square. If he wishes to stop and examine a

38. When there is enough space a conventional projector can be used for individual or small group work. When films are studied under these circumstances, in daylight as part of the ordinary run of work, coat-gatherers can come and go without creating a disturbance.

particular section in detail, 'cold' projection bulbs mean that he can do this without danger of burning the film. And he will need little technical help in all this. Young children can pick up the techniques of handling projection equipment faster often than their teachers. And for those of all ages who fear they will always find those sprockets intractably fiddly, there is now on the market a projection system which takes cassetted full-length films (of at least up to half-an-hour in length).

But if this liberation has greatly increased the value of film for children working by themselves, it doesn't mean that darkness and communal watching are of no educational value. A large, bright screen and a darkened room can be great facilitators of concentration. Psychologists have shown how the removal of distracting stimuli to other senses increases the sensitivity of the one still being stimulated. Moreover, the anonymity of a darkened room means that a child can make the emotional reaction he wants to make without embarrassment. Even 'motor sympathy' is more easily engaged in the dark. Motor sympathy is the term psychologists use to describe the physical component

39. a–d. These children were photographed during a film show with the help of hidden cameras and infrared light. Pictures of this sort reveal just how much muscular activity is involved in watching and responding to a film, and the degrees of concentration which can be achieved at different ages.

of 'identification' with characters and action: the way that the spectator reproduces, on a minute scale, the physical activity happening on the screen. So, when a heavy weight is being lifted in the film, the audience's arm muscles are contracting along with the actors'. With a particular film, then, there may be clear advantages in using a darkened room. There will also be many situations in which a class will benefit from viewing a film *communally*. For instance, when the teacher believes that the feelings expressed by the films should be shared by all the children.

But film has its drawbacks. Although they quickly pass into a stage of visual literacy, very young children don't find the conventions of the cinema at all natural. The size of the image, for instance, is difficult to cope with and the children sometimes fail to relate what is happening on one side of the screen to what is happening on the other. Conversely, the technique of cutting in a film can lead a child to relate too much, and to make some curious conclusions about the chain of cause and effect in the story. Finally, it takes some time before a child can make sense of cinematic language, of symbolic images and tangential reference (e.g. the portrayal of an emergency braking in a car by close-ups of driver's face, hands tightening, and squealing tyres.) Teachers of very young children consequently need to choose films with care, and to be clear about the function they want them to fulfil before deciding whether to show them communally on a large screen or release them for individual use.

One self-educational film aid which is comparatively free from these complications is the film loop. This is a strip of 8mm film, with a running time of between three and four minutes. It is packed into a cassette in such a way that its two ends are joined, enabling it to be projected continuously. The loop is projected in a device similar to the box discussed above. The child simply clips the cassette into the

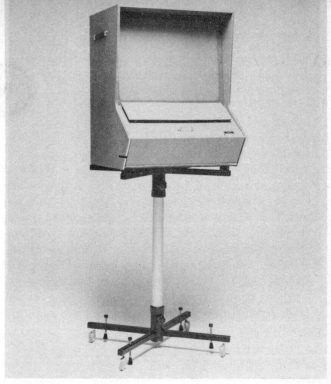

40. An 8mm film-loop projector.

front of the projector and switches on. The image, as before, is thrown on to a ground glass screen.

The film loop is *not* a miniature documentary. There are a few expensive devices for showing sound loops, but in most cases they are silent. This is not a shortcoming but the source of the film loop's particular qualities and usefulness. The film loop began as the 'single-concept loop'. The idea behind it was that there are many notions and operations (particularly in science) which can be reduced to a single pattern or sequence of moving images. In the case of cell division, or a stitch in knitting, a literal representation has the flowing coherence of movement that is the essence of the loop; in the case of a process like the nitrogen cycle, it is a metaphorical, diagrammatic representation that crayons in the circle.

Strong visual ideas of this sort are usually only weakened by the addition of voices (though a teacher electing to show a loop to a whole class may add a subsistence commentary herself). They communicate most effectively by *rhythm*, a quality inherent in all the subjects that go easily into loop form – and indeed in the repetition of the images as the film passes the projection lens for the second and third time. A loop is ideal for showing a mime, a changing cloud formation, a chemical reaction. It is not good for demonstrating a highly complex process, or for filling out action with 'background'. The image's poor definition and shortness of duration make it an inadequate medium for any subject that needs detailing, or which tends to fragment into asides and qualifications.

The physical nature of the film-loop image, and the conceptual singularity of the loops themselves, can make this a particularly valuable medium for those very young children who find difficulty with full-blown films. In fact, the film loop is a classic case of how a medium and a style of subject matter can be matched with one another.

It might be thought that textbook illustrations can now be made so rich and colourful (and large), that there's no longer any place in the classroom for the slide projector. But this is one more case where the machinery may be all-important. Most teachers will confirm that for a child, the act of choosing a slide (or frame from a film-strip), loading it into a projector, and showing it to himself on his private piece of wall, gives the picture he sees more *significance*. The whole operation is riddled with associations from his communications life outside school: the on-switch and the

41. A film-strip sequence showing the defensive camouflage of the hawk-eyed moth. Frames 13 to 16 are using, in effect, the techniques of zooming and jump cutting normally employed in moving pictures.

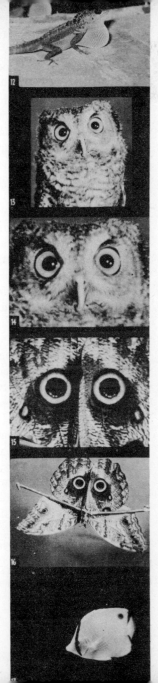

illuminated screen. Psychologically, too, the stage-by-stage mechanics of loading and showing a slide, and the brightness of the image, are good for focusing attention.

There is room for expanding the scope of the film-strip. Christine Vincent in the Picture Research Department at Penguin Education is developing split images, and changes of perspective in consecutive pictures of the same scene, that make the switch from one slide to the next very like a 'cut' in a moving film.

But motivation apart, how effective are slides in communicating information, compared with book illustrations? This is one of the very few areas in the whole audio-visual field in which a piece of *detailed* research has been done.[1] The subjects were a group of French children aged between nine and thirteen. The experiment was carefully constructed and controlled, but consisted basically of the children viewing groups of still photographs and projected slides, and then being asked to 'write on the sheet of paper that has been given to you everything you see in the picture'. In all cases the children observed and recorded substantially more (averaging around fifty per cent) detail from direct examination of a photograph than from projection on a screen.[2]

Now this might be a conclusion we could have anticipated from what we've seen already about how films and books communicate with children. Screened images, beamed *at* the child, tend to make a powerful but generalized emotional impact. Books, which are worked *by* children, can carry greater detail and ideas demanding

1. Fuller details of this experiment are quoted in *The Psychology of the Use of Audio-Visual Aids in Primary Education*, G. Mialaret, Harrap/UNESCO, 1966.

2. An interesting aside on this result was the fact that in all cases girls recalled considerably more details than boys. Is this in accord with the discovery of other surveys that in this age range girls prefer

42. The bright image and regular, 'clicked' picture changes of a film-strip are good focusers of attention. Yet the strip conveys impressions much better than details, and the teacher's comments can be invaluable for filling the latter in.

reflection. But it is not a conclusion which is accepted as part of ordinary classroom practice. Slides are still commonly used on the assumption that their greater image size makes them better at communicating detail to a child.

These points raise a lot of tantalizing questions about the value of slides as self-educational aids. If their usefulness is mainly as attention holders and motivators, how well will they perform in the usual self-educational situation: one corner of a noisy classroom in broad daylight? If on the other hand they are used as the visual element in a lecture to the whole class, how much attention will be left for the teacher's commentary – on which, presumably, will fall the burden of filling in the detail?

*

The paradoxes associated with the use of film-strips and slides exist with all audio-visual aids. They cannot simply be

line-drawings to photographs? I suppose it depends what you mean by detail.

substituted one for another. A film loop does not 'say' the same thing as a wall chart, even if their subject matter is identical. Every piece of hardware has a specific social meaning for the child. Every medium is best suited to the communication of certain sorts of ideas and information. Every type of classroom context modifies the way this communication happens. Even in the most self-educational situation, the teacher's guidance is consequently anything but redundant.

Discovery

If the media can ease along and enrich many of the *processes* of learning, what can they contribute to the achievement of educational ends? Do children learning by themselves ever actually learn anything – apart from, perhaps, how to load a cassette?

There can be no answer to this question which satisfies everybody. What is a legitimate and useful piece of learning to one person is a trivial by-product to another. The *ends* of learning are the subjects of moral, not practical, choices and aren't easy to argue about. For instance, most of us would agree that speaking and reading are invaluable attributes, however they are used. Yet for much of the child's life these are processes through which learning happens, rather than the ends towards which the operation is directed. My own belief is that most learning is of this sort when it's closely scrutinized. Even when teaching is blatantly concerned with content what the child retains is more often in the field of style and method.

Think of maths and science and social studies. Any science teacher would be happy if all her pupils picked up was a respect for evidence and the experimental method; no social studies teacher could hope for more than that her children learned to look at society without prejudice but with compassion. These are ways and means indeed; styles of approach to the problems of learning inside the school and living outside it. But are they any less ends than a knowledge of the properties of water or of the family life of West Indians?

Children's work with the media can be looked at in the same way. Much of the sheer familiarizing process is valuable in its own right. It encourages a healthily critical attitude in the child to the channels of communication through which an increasing amount of his experience is going to come. And there can be little doubt about the value of the learning situations which the media can facilitate. Any child who learns to work independently has made something of his education whatever the quality of that work. But I hope I have not given the impression that the child should not also be helped towards the assimilation of ideas and information. An educationist who takes up the position that adults should give nothing to children but room to grow is not being liberating but constricting. A child would probably just call him selfish.

In various ways the media can help make the child's processes of discovery and independent learning successful. Some ways are more successful than others. We've already seen, for instance, how children remember more details from still photographs than from projected slides. Similarly fine distinctions could be made between all the media. In fact for *any* aid to be of its fullest value, a teacher needs to know with some precision what she wants her children to get out of it. But I want to confine myself here to looking at those general properties of the media that can help the child's independent learning actually come up with the jackpot.

By Encouragement

The only full-length lesson I have ever conducted in a primary school was a blatant piece of media-wielding, hopefully directed towards uncovering a few biological notions. I own a collection of British bird-song records, and a friend whose class of nine-year-olds were hotfoot after birds one summer asked me if I would like to come and play some of them to the children. It was an irresistible invitation, but as it stood, just a little too easy: no child can resist a bittern's boom, or the absurd lavatorial flush at the end of the capercaillie's song. It seemed to me that I ought to try and do a little more than simply play the sounds, and perhaps try and nudge the children into thinking about the function of bird-song.

In the end the experiment didn't turn out too badly. I distributed about half-a-dozen well-illustrated books around the class and allowed plenty of time between announcing the next song and playing the appropriate track, so that the children could look up each bird and examine its picture at the same time as listening to its song. On the school's hi-fi the songs came over stunningly.

But I began without the records, by asking the children to listen to what was going on in the school grounds. It was September, so there was virtually no song. Why not? Most of the children already associated bird-song with spring, so we got to the relation between song and nesting fairly quickly. But what was the song *for*? 'Because they like the warm weather.' 'To attract a mate.' 'So the babies know they are there.' Not even professional biologists would pour the scorn on these answers that they might have done a few years ago, and I didn't want to discuss them until we had listened to some song. But there was one piece of information I did have to hand them, since we weren't in the field observation business, and that was the fact that normally only male birds *sing* (though all birds call).

Then we had some records, first of very loud singers. The children regarded finding the right pictures as a challenge. They all knew the wren was small and were surprised at the loudness of its song. The bittern's boom, I told them, carried half a mile. Where did bitterns sing from? Hidden amongst the reeds, they found by some rapid scanning of the texts. Then I switched to poor singers: the brilliantly-coloured kingfisher, and the more aggressive hawks. They gradually began to see the pattern that in general the small, dull, shy birds were the loudest bawlers, and the brightly plumaged, conspicuous ones the poorest. Some of the children offered solutions to this. They were 'showing off', 'sticking up for themselves'. We recapped. Bird-song was male birds showing off during the breeding season. One boy remembered that blackbirds and thrushes usually sang from the same perch on spring evenings. Were they saying 'This is where I live'? We had arrived at a rough notion of territory, and at this point I felt it was worth explaining in some detail that this was the most popular theory about why birds sang.

Admittedly it was a fairly structured lesson and I have little doubt that an observer would have noticed more unconscious prompting on my part than I care to remember. But I think that the media have certain characteristics that make this sort of discovery-learning fairly natural and commonplace.

Learning by discovery in real life happens when children are faced with some sort of problem which needs to be resolved – be the reasons survival or the satisfaction of an inquisitive spirit. Formal education in school has to consist of the construction of artificial problems which, whilst they will often lack the imperatives of real life, may raise in their solution more generally useful skills and concepts. The best teaching strategies in this area – and the Nuffield Science Teaching Projects must be numbered amongst these – seek to make their components enriching to the child even if he fails to draw the conclusions for which they were originally chosen.

The media can help enormously here. They are the main agencies for bringing remote real-life experiences into the classroom. To the degree to which they can do this with a certain amount of authenticity, they don't necessarily cut off a child's purely imaginative or sensory response to the experience: my children will probably remember the barn owl's screech much longer than any high-flown ethological ideas. But on the other hand the media's capacity for compressing time and space means that they can structure experience in ways that could only happen by chance in the first-hand world.

An alternative to the media is to structure the environment itself. This is less like social engineering than it sounds. In biology – to stay with the example I've already used – it simply produces the Nature Trail. These will scarcely need any introduction, so many are now being created round power stations, reservoirs and other improbable patches of urban wasteland. But their capacity for transforming, translating and structuring experience has much in common with the media: take a rich and varied location, pick out a handful of key, expressive situations and guide your audience past them. Bring the whole thing indoors to a Nature Centre with animal tracks painted on the floor and brief flashes of birds on film on the wall, and you are back in straightforward media country.

By Decree

In situations where there is little scope for the child's imagination, and the end desired is simply his arrival at a fixed goal by the most efficient and most persuasive route, then programmed learning can be of great use. The number of occasions when this sort of end is desirable in the primary age range are limited, which is why there is so far very little programmed material available. Yet programmes are self-instructional, and have from time to time been offered inside some outlandish pieces of machinery, so I think I should mention them here.

Programmes are usually written on cards or in books, and they have three essential features. First, the material to be taught must be broken down into small, easily assimilable units, which are then presented in carefully thought-out sequence. In this way they don't differ from a well-prepared lecture. Secondly, they test the learning of each unit *immediately* after it has been presented. But again, any trained teacher knows the value of instant reinforcement, be it correction or reward; and though teaching in this way may not always be practicable, at her Socratic best she can deal it out, and give more personalized rewards into the bargain. The third and only special virtue of teaching programmes takes us really back to the book: they do require the child to play an *active* role. Although to a sceptical eye they may appear as nothing more than scripts of teacher/child dialogue, to a child they offer at least the impression of more dignified and independent work than any exchange with a teacher. In the latter situation he is always the responder, never the mover. With a teaching programme he can work by himself, at his own rate, and with each correct response have the delicious feeling of having made the discovery for

111

himself, not having simply 'caught it' from the teacher. I thought for some time about whether the programme's worth as a self-instructional aid meant that it should be more properly discussed in the relevant earlier section. But I think that its particular contribution lies in its capacity to give a child the sense of creatively discovering his way through a topic.

Of course, it is someone else's path and someone else's answer he is being led to 'discover'. Which is why teaching programmes must be constructed and used with the very greatest care, particularly in primary schools. There are two main forms which can be called on. The linear programme breaks its ideas and information into very small stages indeed, small enough to guarantee almost every child a right answer every time. The branching programme is less concerned about the weight of its sections, and places a multiple-choice question after each one. If the child responds correctly he is congratulated and led on to the next section. If he chooses a wrong answer he is taken along a remedial path where the nature and possible cause of his error are explained. Although the branching programme is somewhat more open-ended than the linear, they are both ultimately concerned with convergency. This is the way they teach. They impress knowledge most efficiently when the child makes no mistakes at all, but follows the tight central thread of the programme from tick to tick. They are only really excusable as tools, therefore, when the subject for teaching is seen to be one where the child's contribution will be negligible if not downright diverting. For the technique of using a microscope or the laws concerning stealing they can be invaluable primers; but for the structure of living matter and the *reasons* for law they could, with young children, be positively dangerous.

For this reason some of the best work with programmes

43. The Bell & Howell Language Master. Beneath the phonetically written words there is a strip of twin-track tape, one track carrying the sound of the word, the other open for the child to record his own version. The bar above the microphone enables the child to switch tracks, and compare his own version of the word with the pre-recorded sound.

has been done in language teaching. Any number of systems have been devised using combinations of tape, film-strips, word-cards and even typewriters. At their simplest these programmes try to build up a carefully graded vocabulary by showing the child a word (and perhaps the object to which it refers) at the same time as he hears it on the tape. Soon afterwards the word crops up on the tape again, and the child will be instructed to pick out the card on which it is written. The language laboratory itself is a classic example of programming theory in practice. Spoken language is presented in small, carefully graded sections on a tape. There are pauses after each section in which the listener records his own version of what the speaker has said, or fills in words which he should have learned by this stage. The pupil can then play back his own version and have 'instant reinforcement' by comparing his interpretation with the original.

Mention of these language devices brings us to the teaching machine, unnecessarily nightmarish in so many

113

44. Discovering your own voice. A language-laboratory system especially devised for deaf children.

45. The Autotutor teaching machine. The buttons down the right-hand edge of the machine correspond to the possible answers to multiple-choice questions, and move the programme (which is shot on 35mm film) on to further frames which correct wrong choices and provide new information.

teachers' and parents' eyes. Teaching machines are nothing more than mechanical devices for presenting written programmes in a tidy, step-by-step sequence to the pupil. The arguments about their merits and defects have been vehement over the past few years. But it now looks as if they are largely irrelevant to the success or otherwise of a programme. As intriguing gadgets they no doubt have a certain motivating potential with young children. But the most sophisticated, which look like television sets and have irresistible rows of on-off buttons, are impossibly expensive, especially when you remember that they can only ever be used by one child at a time. The cheaper ones are really rather Heath Robinson, and their attraction for children quickly palls. At their worst they are an uneasy amalgam of the crisp world of machines, and the more relaxed, flexible medium of the printed word. The most persuasive argument in favour of the machines is that they can make the programmes 'cheatproof'; that is, by some mechanical device they can prevent the child from seeing the answer to a question until he has had a shot at finding it for himself. But knowing that cheating can be a most effective form of instant reinforcement for many children, perhaps this is the point at which we should leave the teaching machine.

Co-operation

Between Children

Cheating of course is most educationally valuable when it takes the form of the willing sharing of knowledge between

46.

children of differing abilities. When this happens it is more than the answer that is being passed on.

The media play an important role in mixed-ability work in ·the primary school. Whether they are being used actively or passively they capitalize on all sorts of skills which a predominantly literary culture tends to overlook. And with their capacity to facilitate independent learning they allow children to contribute at their own level to the work of the group. In one passage of the book I quoted from earlier, Stuart Froome criticizes publicity photographs of this sort of work with these revealing words:

Now in all these pictures, which are obviously posed for a good photographer, the number of children at work rarely exceeds five or six. This tempts the average primary school teacher to pose the question, 'Where are the other thirty-five?' Perhaps they are absent sick, or maybe they are in another part of the building being taken by a traditional formal type of teacher who was not chosen as part of the progressive Plowden propaganda.[1]

The answer is nothing like as devious as Stuart Froome suggests. Most of the children will be in precisely similar groups of five and six in various corners of the classroom,

1. *Why Tommy Isn't Learning*, Stuart Froome, Tom Stacey Books, 1970.

47. A propaganda picture for the progressive primary school. The other thirty-five children are on pages 15, 24, etc.

reading, listening to tapes, watching films and generally proving that they are quite capable of working co-operatively without the constant supervision of the teacher.

It is the fact that most of the media are inherently co-operative that gives them their special value in this sort of work. Many primary schools now own cine cameras, for instance, and use the making of a film as the culmination of a group or class project. Whether it's a fictional story to be acted, or a documentary on the insects in the school ground, the exercise of making a film involves accountancy, tea-making, electronics, the physics of light, timetabling,

48. Making animated films can be a natural extension of children's work in art.

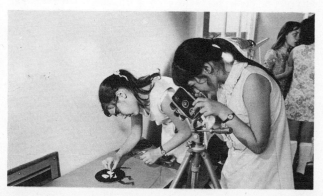

make-up, writing, and public relations. Any child, whatever his abilities or interests, can find a niche in an operation of this sort. He will not only get valuable experience in developing the particular skill for which he is being employed, but also in team work. One city school I know sends teams of young children out on location filming in wild countryside. Another buys reject stock from cutting rooms and allows the children to experiment on editing. (Apparently the results are discomfortingly unsentimental.)

Closed-circuit television is another eminently co-operative medium. In spite of the high cost of the equipment one or two primary schools already have the necessary cameras and recorders to put together their own programmes. I saw a videotape which one class made on the subject of water. They had planned and written their own script, made the models and diagrams and chosen two startlingly articulate boys to present the programme. The attitude of these children towards the equipment is terrifying to a teacher with one eye on next year's budget, but revealing none the less. They see it as a useful tool, nothing more, certainly not something deserving respect, wonder and a delicate touch. They handle it confidently but roughly. It may figure in the education authority's equipment list, but it is the children's world to which it really belongs. They can pick up the essential stages in operating a camera or videotape recorder in an afternoon. Some of them even learn how to make small running repairs on the equipment.

A booklet put out by the National Committee for Audiovisual Aids in Education gives this fascinating account of the use of closed-circuit TV by an infants class:

Back in their classrooms, or at break-time in the playground, the children brooded and gossiped over the possibilities. Then they streamed back, in ones and twos, in syndicates of four or five, in production groups of fifteen or twenty. They developed

49.

their ideas and concerted their plans wherever it suited them best: sometimes in their classrooms, sometimes in the *studio floor* of the assembly hall. Their teachers, as usual, were on hand to give guidance, answer queries, reconcile conflicting personalities, reassure the timid; but we had agreed beforehand that no adult should intervene unasked, with ideas, or organization. In fact no one needed to. The children were self-propelled – and self-directed. They knew what they wanted: one very small boy squatting to give a recital of home-made drumming; a girl reading aloud a story she had written and illustrated, holding her book so that the camera could show up the handwriting as well as the pictures; a group of clowns in home-made red noses; four acrobats vaulting and balancing on boxes strategically placed to give the cameras the appropriate vantage points . . .

In a later session with the same class. A boy brought in a dead bird, magnified it on the screen, and began to use a second camera, on the drawing frame, to sketch out a drawing of the wing skeleton. A girl followed the movements of a live stag beetle, and without any prompting drew it, wrote about it, demanded a microphone and presented illustrations and live shots to her own spoken commentary. Meanwhile the children were shown how the frame and its underneath mirror could be used as a silhouetting device, and how the silhouettes could be made to move. Suddenly everyone seemed to be cutting out men and animals in black card to try out. The floor provided cutting-out and pasting-up space when there were no table tops left. Then some children brought in a dolls' house they had made, and the

119

camera was allowed to wander over it, making the matchbox beds and the matchstick chairs seem life-size. Suddenly the place came alive to them. They began an endless story about the house and the people who lived there. More models and building layouts were brought in and explored afresh. Handwriting and number-work were looked at. A backward reader with a disturbed home background recruited a more able friend to help him and began dictating a story. The friend wrote the words down so that they could be copied. As each sentence was completed the sheet was taken to the writing frame to be shown on 'telly', and as the story took shape the author began to add his cut-outs and animate them as he read aloud the story he had written.[1]

It is important to remember that most of these children were only six years old. Yet they assimilated this complicated equipment completely into their natural, 'childlike' ways of working. It is revealing that when the teachers of this class tried to organize the work along tidier adult lines, the results were disastrous:

. . . we all agreed that it was about time to *structure* the situation a little. The children were asked to take turns to show their work, on the television screen, to the other groups involved. We remembered the previous experiment and the attention the children gave to achieving a performance. Perhaps this demanded an audience to give things shape. But we were wrong, it seemed. That afternoon the whole thing fell flat. The presentation was stilted, the zest had gone. Next day we went back to the seemingly disorganized flurry of activity, and the thing came alive again. Once more the subject matter, and the children's own intention regarding it, took command; they lost themselves in their work; what seemed to matter was not how it appeared to other people, but how it measured up, when the tape was replayed, to each individual's or each group's particular vision.[2]

One of the more remarkable features of the videotape on

1. Extracts from *Experiments in Television*, Tony Gibson, NCAVE, 1968.
2. ibid.

50.

water I studied was the personality of the producer. He had been, by all accounts, a rather slow-witted child, generally unmotivated and slow to pick up in conventional academic areas. Yet the combination of administrative ability and visual flair needed for this job had transformed him. He had shown abilities which neither he nor his teachers could have anticipated – and won the respect of the other children in the process.

Pooling Resources

We have come back to one of our starting points. Just as each child gives to the work of a group his own particular skill, so each section of the community can make its own contribution to the work of the school. One of the happiest days I have ever spent in a primary school was in a small market town in Oxfordshire. It was an idyllically hot summer's afternoon, and it was the day the Morris Dancer came. He was no gaudily decked professional but a traveller in agricultural products who popped into the local schools between calls. He just tied red ribbons round his salesman's trousers, pulled out a couple of handkerchiefs and began. The children drifted in from the school grounds where many

121

51. She is a TV star. She may never have done anything exceptional at school before, but now she has a chance to speak to her fellow pupils through the most prestigious of all media. The effect of this responsibility can transform a child's attitude to school work.

of them had been listening to stories read by parent volunteers, and sat down, delighted. In minutes they were dancing too.

The media expand enormously the number of outsiders who can contribute to school life in this way. Photography, for instance, can be a channel through which parents can help. Cine films and holiday snaps can be highly motivating with children, given the flavour they carry of reflecting a *friend's* experiences.

None of this in any way implies that the class teacher is becoming redundant. Her role is what it always was: she is the person who deals directly with the children. In the primary school at least, children are her speciality; the subject comes second. All the media do is to vastly increase the range of material which she can manage and present to the child, and as we have seen, the range of situations in which he can experience it. No one can play this role satisfactorily for the teacher, just as she cannot really provide the same service as many of the outside agencies. The best possible situation is where every party in the relationship between school and the outside world is *doing what they can do best:* lecturers, museums, film-makers, dancers, broadcasting companies, and teachers.

This is not to say that there are not many services being provided from the outside that could now be equally well provided by the school. Any school, for instance, that possesses an 8mm camera can make its own film loops – and consequently tailor them very closely to its own needs. The advances in cheap techniques of copying and reproducing documents mean that a teachers' centre – if not a school

52. Overhead projector transparencies, which can be easily made up with Letraset or felt-pen work, are ideal examples of the sorts of material best produced by teachers themselves.

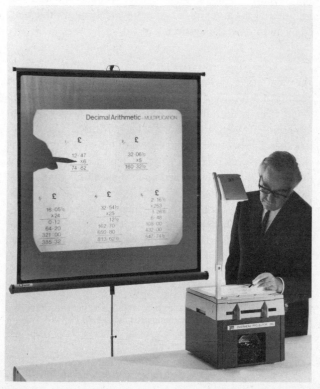

– can now print its own publications. The graphic quality of material set by electric typewriter may not be quite up to Eric Gill standards, but it will usually be good enough for its own purposes.

Again, 'doing what you can do best' is the key. Where local detailing and individual tailoring are more important than 'finish', a teachers' centre or well-equipped school is by far the best source of material; where an expensive actor or a full-colour book is needed and some sort of national distribution desired, a commercial company is probably better suited to the job. The result could be a bipolar structure of materials production: 'cottage industry' production of bespoke local materials, based around the bigger schools and teachers' centres, and national production and distribution of more complex and more widely applicable materials by commercial agencies.[1]

*

The final stage of any project in a primary school is the making of a record of what has been done or what has been found. This is desirable not just because it gives the child something to work towards, and helps focus and clarify his thinking, but because a solid record of his work can give the child a sense of pride in what he has done. His work is *significant*. If it can be pinned up or played back on parents' day, so much the better.

Again, the media expand the range of channels through which children can express the results of their work. If previously they could paint or write or make collections, they can now make a film or tape documentary as well. Still photography could be one of the great growth areas here.

1. Even the Dairy Industry is currently running a Project Club. For less than a pound and six extra pints of milk you get a manual containing '240 colourful pages with hundreds of projects'.

With a hundred million pounds a year being spent on amateur photography, the snapshot looks like taking over the role of the diary entry and the letter.

Part Three

*Postscript — The Primary School and the
Outside World*

This book has been chiefly concerned with the contributions the media can make towards the patterns of work current in primary schools. We've seen how they can confront the child with new human and physical experiences; how they can facilitate both solitary work and group co-operation; and how one of the avenues of this co-operation is between the school and the community. To this extent it is an optimistic account. Many teachers and parents may view the descriptions of children working which I have given above as hopelessly idealistic, and based on a small minority of atypical schools. Well, based on a minute sample of schools the documentary accounts inevitably are; but they are only atypical to the degree that many schools have not yet had the opportunity – or the financial resources – to take advantage of the new media. The children themselves, whatever some of their teachers may fear, seem to feel natural and affectionate in the presence of the media, yet offer them nothing so ingratiating as respect. They are not 'dehumanized', nor are the vital qualities of their schools challenged in any way. For children *play* with the media as they do with paint and tadpoles, with the same concern for understanding and the same indifference to technique. If we are looking for a villain that does challenge these special qualities of childhood it is surely not the new machines, but the old patterns of rigid, passive learning.

A young American sociologist gave a considerable insight into the role of the media in children's lives, when, explain-

53, 54.

ing the appeal of pop musicians to the young, he said: 'They work when they play, and play when they work.' The twin meanings of the word 'play' implied in this quote are obvious in the way that children manipulate the media. They play with them at the same time as playing on them. Enjoyment and rehearsal are practised simultaneously with personal communication. We can see the same process at work in any adventure playground as the children transform the abandoned débris of our industrial society into an environment for their adventures and fantasies.

130

55. The proper use of technology. It is fitting that children know how to transform the derelict remains of adult artefacts into a world of freedom and excitement.

But I think the special gift of the media is the broadening of the pattern of relationships between children, teachers and the outside world. 'Media' could be short for 'mediators': like speech they are channels for communication between humans, and as such can bring them into relationships. What we have discussed so far has mostly concerned communication from the community to the school. But we should not forget that it can be the other way round, from the school to the community. Much of this happens at a very practical level, by, say, the loaning out of the school buildings and equipment. The children can also conduct censuses, make surveys of local river pollution, and, specifically in the field of the media, help with the production and testing of films and tapes for other schools. And is it entirely out of place to mention here those primary school paintings that are now used to adorn the TV weather forecasts? The genuine public use of his work is the greatest tribute which can be paid to a young child.

But perhaps the gifts of the primary school to the world at large are most important when they are less tangible than this. I spoke above about 'transformation'. Play can be transforming because it is essentially a redefinition of the nature of an object or situation. So is the use of the media in primary schools, which has been an object lesson in how to make technology your servant rather than your master. In its own small way the primary school, helped by communications technology, is learning how to put into practice ideas we only pay lip-service to in the outside world: how to build a democratic community in which people of all ages, backgrounds and abilities can co-operate – both face to face and at a distance. We, on the outside, mourning the loss of our childishness and sense of community, could do worse than to watch these places closely.

guard
against mum
and that axe

by NICHOLAS HARLING

GREEN FINGERED Simon Wray is keeping a careful watch on his mother these days.

For Mrs Frances Hutchinson, the woman who adopted ten-year-old Simon, his two brothers and sisters, is threatening to chop down his 12-feet high sunflower plant.

The trouble is that the six-week-old plant outside the Hutchinson's home in Watermans Close, Watford,

is a sunflower without flowers.

"It's a monstrosity," complained Mrs Hutchinson. "I am going out one night to chop it down, and I will pretend the wind blew it down."

Simon's 12-year-old s Frances her mi

For throu wind

"

a'

Picture: MIC

56.

Picture Acknowledgements

Title Page: John Walmsley

PLATES

1., 2. John Walmsley
2. *The Times*
4. *Astrad Orion*
5. Photo: Doisneau – Rapho
6. Albertina, Vienna
7. John Walmsley
8. Jane Bown
9., 10. Euan Duff
11. John Walmsley
12., 13., 14. British Petroleum Co. Ltd
16. G.L.C. Library
17. John Walmsley
18. Penguin Education Illustration Department
19. Dr Harold E. Edgerton
20. Illustromat

21. John Walmsley
22.
23., 25. I.P.S.
26. B.B.C. Photo Library
28. Oxford City Museum
29. Patrick Ward
30., 32. John Walmsley
37. Evans Brothers Ltd
38. John Walmsley
40. Guild Holdings Ltd
41. Photography Lilo Hess
42., 43. John Walmsley
44. Maria Bartha
45. John Walmsley
46. Euan Duff
47., 48., 51. John Walmsley
52. Freddie Squires Ltd
53., 54. John Walmsley
55. Maria Bartha

Index

Penguin Primary Project

Over the past ten years there have been more exciting ideas coming out of the British primary school than perhaps any other single educational institution in the world. It has been realized that, given an environment of sympathetic adults and rich materials, any child is capable of quite remarkable achievements.

The PENGUIN PRIMARY PROJECT is a programme of materials designed to make a major contribution to this environment of information and stimuli inside which children work. Its organization is straightforward: clusters of books, records and audio-visual material arranged in Units around basic themes.

The Project directors have throughout thrown emphasis on quality and flexibility. The Units as far as possible cross the traditional disciplinary bounds; and they use the best professional advice to provide problems and topics which stimulate thought and discussion. Suggestions for experimental work have been incorporated, together with stimulating passages for reading and a multitude of full-colour illustrations provided with simple but intelligent captions or comments for group work or personal study.

Two Units are now available, *Your Body* and *Communications*, which are described in more detail in the following pages.

Penguin Primary Project

Your Body

Edited by Ted Orsborn

BOOKS

LARGE AS LIFE   *Gillian Evans*

The human body in art. Introduces such concepts as
stereotyping, distortion, and abstraction.

LIVING AND MEASURING   *Marc Goldstein*

A wholly original approach to maths via the child's
experience of the dimensions of his own body.

SAFE AND SOUND   *Sonya Leff*

The human body in illness, and what can be done to
protect it.

ON THE MOVE   *Raymond Rivers*

Movement, both internal and external, is one of the
chief characteristics of living creatures. This book,
cutting across social, biological and physical sciences,
looks at the human body 'on the move'.

BEGINNINGS   *Harry Thomas*

How the human body got the way it is. The stories of the
evolution of the human species and of the individual
human infant told in parallel.

also available

TEACHERS' HANDBOOK

STANDARD 8 FILM ON REELS

INSIDES Colour film taken by cine X-ray and micro-photography of heart-beating, peristalsis in the gut, blood cell movement, cell division and the ingestion of bacteria.

OUTSIDES The capacity of the human body to make movement both efficient and beautiful. Illustrated in colour by shots of ballet dancing, athletics, writing, showing the contrasts between strength and delicacy.

(Both also available on film loops)

FILM STRIP

THE WAY I FEEL TODAY The everyday experience of our own and others' bodies. Growing up with them, learning to use them, and to 'read' what they express.

Two 7" 33⅓ records are also available

Heartbeats and Mouthmusic – exploring the internal and external sounds of the body.

Working and Dancing – an imaginative insight into the rhythms of human life.

Penguin Primary Project

Communications

Edited by Edward Goldwyn and Philippa Harverson

BOOKS

LOOK WHAT I'VE MADE   *Geoffrey Summerfield*

A book more of pictures than of words, about the
borderline between communication and art: the ways
we interpret, talk about and celebrate the world
around us.

SIGNS AND SIGNALS   *Philippa Harverson*

The basic elements of language systems, what they
mean and how they work.

MACHINES AND MESSAGES   *Sylvia Caveney*

Machines for communicating. The way that technology
has vastly expanded the ways we can communicate
with each other – and the problems this has raised.

KEEPING TRACK   *Sylvia Caveney*

Storage is now an important part of communication.
This book looks at the principles behind, and
techniques of, information storage. Includes
experiments such as the building of a simple computer.

also available

TEACHERS' HANDBOOK

STANDARD 8 FILM ON REELS

THE ACCIDENT A colour film testing the fallibility of perception and memory. Two girls, a driver, his son and his dog and perhaps other people, are involved in a near-accident. We are witnesses to the events leading up to it. But do we see, remember and interpret the events correctly?

LOOK, NO WORDS! Communicating without words. A colour film in which Julian Chagrin, Britain's foremost mime expert, tells two tales in mime.

(*Both also available on film loops*)

FILM STRIPS

ANIMAL SIGNALS Communicative signals in the animal world: mimicry, courtship displays, camouflage, etc.

PUTTING IDEAS IN YOUR HEAD The use and impact of graphics in posters and advertisements, particularly those aimed at children.

Two 7" 33⅓ records are also available

Finding Your Voice – an exploration of the meaning of sounds, in life and in fiction.

Talking English – the development and current dialects of the English language.

Penguin Education

Take Part Books

Adapted by Sheila Lane and Marion Kemp

The books in the series are well-known children's books abridged into dialogue form. Each character in the story has a part written out at a particular reading level, so that groups of children can therefore read the books together, each child taking part at a level suitable to his ability.

These books provide stimulating group reading material within the school and the home. Parents can do much to motivate their children towards reading for pleasure by taking part themselves.

The unique qualities of the *Take Part Books* are that they
■ provide motivation and experience in reading for the 6 to 9+ range
■ enable each child to practise and develop reading techniques at his own level
■ give the child a feeling of contributing to a useful collaborative venture
■ can be used with a minimum of supervision leaving the teacher free to teach specific techniques to groups within the class
■ have been tested extensively and with favourable results

BEAVERBIRD from the story by Ruth Underhill

CHITTY-CHITTY-BANG-BANG from the story by Ian Fleming

FOLK TALES from the stories by Leila Berg

PARSLEY AND HERBS from the stories by Michael Bond

THE TREASURE SEEKERS from the story by E. Nesbit

THE WIND IN THE WILLOWS from the story by Kenneth Grahame

THE WIZARD OF OZ from the story by L. F. Baum